BETTER THAN HUMAN

PHILOSOPHY IN ACTION
Small Books about Big Ideas

Walter Sinnott-Armstrong, series editor

BETTER THAN HUMAN

The Promise and Perils of Enhancing Ourselves

Allen Buchanan

OXFORD
UNIVERSITY PRESS

Oxford University Press, Inc., publishes works that further
Oxford University's objective of excellence
in research, scholarship, and education.

Oxford   New York
Auckland   Cape Town   Dar es Salaam   Hong Kong   Karachi
Kuala Lumpur   Madrid   Melbourne   Mexico City   Nairobi
New Delhi   Shanghai   Taipei   Toronto

With offices in
Argentina   Austria   Brazil   Chile   Czech Republic   France   Greece
Guatemala   Hungary   Italy   Japan   Poland   Portugal   Singapore
South Korea   Switzerland   Thailand   Turkey   Ukraine   Vietnam

Published by Oxford University Press, Inc.
198 Madison Avenue, New York, New York 10016

www.oup.com

Oxford is a registered trademark of Oxford University Press

Library of Congress Cataloging-in-Publication Data
Buchanan, Allen E., 1948–
Better than human: the promise and perils of biomedical enhancement/ Allen Buchanan.
    p.   cm.—(Philosophy in action) (Small books about big ideas)
Includes bibliographical references.
ISBN 978-0-19-979787-5 (alk. paper)
1. Bioethics.   2. Medical innovations—Moral and ethical aspects.   I. Title.   II. Series.
QH332.B83 2011
174.2—dc22   2010052276

1 3 5 7 9 8 6 4 2

Printed in the United States of America
on acid-free paper

PREFACE

I recently published a much longer scholarly book, also with Oxford University Press, on the ethics of biomedical enhancement, entitled *Beyond Humanity?* That book was written for a more academic audience and was especially directed toward professional bioethicists and moral philosophers. Because I believe that the themes it explored are of great public interest, I've written the present volume with a wider audience in mind.

The present volume contains no footnotes, though it does have an extensive bibliography. For those who desire documentation for what I say in this book, I suggest you look at the scholarly book. It contains a mind-numbing expanse of endnotes.

Better than Human isn't a dumbed-down version of *Beyond Humanity?* It includes a number of ideas that occurred to me after *Beyond Humanity?* was already in press. Nonetheless, *Better than Human* is considerably leaner than its predecessor. I've eliminated some rather complex and some might say arcane discussions that are appropriate for scholars but guaranteed to induce deep sleep in normal people.

In addition to having somewhat different content, the two books are written in quite different styles. The present volume is more informal and conversational. And, I might add, it more directly expresses my feelings about the topic and about how it is often presented and discussed.

Because this book builds on its predecessor, I should acknowledge all those who helped me to write the first volume. I won't repeat the entire list included in the acknowledgments of *Beyond*

Humanity? But I do want to offer special thanks to Matthew Braddock and Whitney Kane for their excellent research assistance and to Sandy Arneson, Jeff L. Holzgrefe, and Russell Powell for their valuable comments on the penultimate draft of *Better than Human.* I also am indebted to Peter Ohlin of OUP and to Walter Sinnot-Armstrong, the outstanding editor of the Philosophy in Action series.

July 25, 2010

CONTENTS

BETTER THAN HUMAN

BREATHLESS OPTIMISM,
HYSTERICAL LOATHING

It's too late to "just say no" to biomedical enhancements: They're already here and more are on the way. Consider the case of Michelle, a bright, ambitious junior at an elite U.S. university. To study more efficiently, Michelle takes Ritalin, a drug prescribed for ADD (attention deficit disorder), though she doesn't have ADD. Ritalin is only one of several drugs developed to treat disorders—including ADD, Alzheimer's dementia, and narcolepsy—that have been shown to improve thinking in people who aren't cognitively impaired. We already have cognitive enhancement drugs, and they are already widely used as such.

Michelle's boyfriend Carlos tells her she shouldn't take Ritalin. He says, "It's cheating and besides it might be dangerous." Michelle replies: "Calm down. It's just a cognitive enhancement drug—a chemical that helps me think better—it's not cocaine. Don't be hypocritical. You take a cognitive enhancement drug, too—probably in dangerously high doses—namely, caffeine. And don't think you're fooling me. You say you've quit, but I know you sneak a cigarette now and then when you're up late studying. I can smell it in your hair. Look, caffeine and nicotine both help you stay alert and think more clearly; that's why so many people use them. So if I'm cheating, so are you and a lot of other people. Besides, if you're worried about unfair advantages, why pick on cognitive enhancement drugs? Just being at this university gives us a huge advantage. What do you think education is? It's cognitive enhancement. Or what about the fact that both your parents are really smart and have PhDs? That's certainly an advantage, too, and you didn't earn it. If I ever have kids, I want them to have the best opportunities I can provide for them. If this means making sure they've got good genes, then so be it. Biomedical enhancement? I'm all for it!"

"Wait a minute," Carlos protests. "Cognitive enhancement drugs, maybe. But now you're talking about genetically designing your children? It's one thing to use a drug to bring out a person's full potential. That's different from changing their nature, making them a different person than they would have been. That's playing God."

I've changed the names, filled out a few incomplete sentences, and corrected for the annoying tendency of undergraduates to punctuate every other phrase with "like." But otherwise this dialogue captures the gist of an exchange between two students in my class on the ethics of biomedical enhancement at Duke University.

Cognitive enhancement drugs are only the beginning. Biomedical science is producing new knowledge at an astounding rate—knowledge that will enable us, if we choose, to transform ourselves. Biomedical enhancements can make us smarter, have better memories, be stronger and quicker, have more stamina, live much longer, be more resistant to disease and to the frailties of aging, and enjoy richer emotional lives. They may even improve our character or at least strengthen our powers of self-control. Enhancement drugs are only part of the story. There's mounting evidence, including successful gene changes in laboratory animals, that human beings will eventually be able to change their physical, cognitive, and emotional capacities by deliberately modifying their genes. Eventually, we might even be able to take charge of human evolution.

A bit of terminology is in order. An *enhancement* is an intervention—a human action of any kind—that improves some capacity (or characteristic) that normal human beings ordinarily have or, more radically, that produces a new one. Cognitive enhancements increase normal cognitive capacities. Cognitive capacities include memory (of which there are several kinds), attention, reasoning, and what psychologists call "executive function," the ability of the mind to monitor, direct, and coordinate various mental operations. A *biomedical* enhancement uses biotechnology to cause an improvement of an existing capacity by acting directly on the body (including the brain).

Biomedical enhancements are contrasted with therapy, defined as the treatment or prevention of diseases. Modifying the genes of a human embryo to prevent a genetic disease would be therapy, not enhancement. Modifying an embryo to improve the normal immune system's capacity for fighting infections would be an enhancement. If we think of disease as an adverse departure from normal functioning, and therapy as aimed at preventing or curing disease, then the contrast with enhancement is clear: Enhancement aims to augment or improve normal functioning. In that sense, it aims to go beyond therapy.

Biomedical enhancements can be sorted out in two ways: according to the *type* of capacity they aim to improve, and according to the *mode* of intervention, the technology they use to improve the capacity. The types of capacities that biomedical enhancements can improve include cognitive function; physical strength, speed, and stamina; mood, temperament, and emotional functioning; and longevity. Enhanced longevity could be achieved either by bolstering the normal immune system to make us less vulnerable to diseases that shorten our lives or, more radically, by counteracting the normal processes by which cells age and eventually fail to regenerate.

The modes of biomedical enhancement include drugs; selecting which embryos to implant in the uterus by screening them for genes that are likely to result in better than normal capacities; implanting genetically altered tissue into the body or brain; genetically engineering human embryos (fertilized egg cells) or gametes (sperm or egg cells); and technologies that connect computers directly to the brain. All of these types and modes of biomedical enhancement have already been used successfully in laboratory animals, and some have been used in humans. Brain/computer interface technologies, for example, are already helping people who have lost their sight or their ability to move their limbs.

Before we go any further, I have to emphasize a simple point. An enhancement is an improvement of some particular capacity, but not necessarily something that makes us better off *overall*. For example, if your hearing were greatly enhanced, it might not improve your life. It might make you miserable, because you might not be able to concentrate due to all the noise. That's why it is better to talk about enhancing capacities rather than enhancing people. If we make the mistake of thinking that enhancing capacities makes us better off overall, we'll also mistakenly think, "Of course we should enhance—better is good!"

Even when an enhancement would make you better off overall, it doesn't follow that you should undertake it. Sometimes, the right thing to do isn't the thing that improves your own situation—especially if doing so wrongly disadvantages someone else or if the improvement comes at the cost of violating some important moral rule or has the effect of undermining your character.

The Michelle-Carlos dialogue encapsulates many of the issues about biomedical enhancement this book will explore. I want to tease out two of them right now. The rest will be examined in subsequent chapters.

The first is that as a society we face a choice between *front door* and *back door* biomedical enhancement. Biomedical enhancement comes through the front door when it makes its appearance as enhancement. This would occur, for example, if the Food and Drug Administration approved drugs that were designed for improving normal memory and were marketed as such. At present, biomedical enhancements don't come through the front door. They come through the back door, as spin-offs of efforts to treat diseases or disorders. That's true in Michelle's case. Ritalin is marketed and prescribed as a treatment for ADD, not as a cognitive enhancement drug. Michele can get her Ritalin in three ways. She can read the Wikipedia article on ADD, memorize the symptoms, and then tell the doctor at the student health clinic that she has them; she can "borrow" or buy the drug from somebody whose doctor prescribed it for him; or she can order it online from a virtual doctor (with some risk of getting a Ritalin knockoff or a watered down dose of the real thing).

There are lots of other cases where what begins as a treatment for a disease becomes an enhancement. Drugs called SSRIs (selective serotonin reuptake inhibitors), the most well-known of which is Prozac, were first developed to treat the disorder of clinical depression. But now millions of people who aren't clinically depressed take them to feel better. (In fact, my vet tells me that people ask her to prescribe it to their perfectly normal dogs to make them more cheerful.) Viagra was developed to treat EDD (erectile dysfunction disorder), but now lots of young men (including Carlos) take it so that they can perform like the Energizer Bunny, even when they're drunk. (Perhaps the most brilliant marketing strategy of recent times is the warning "If you experience an erection lasting more than four hours, seek medical attention.")

Sometimes people seek treatment and get enhancement as an unexpected bonus. For example, the latest high-tech prosthetics for people who have lost a leg actually increase the capacity for rapid running—so much so that there is a movement to ban them from competitions. A few years ago, I had laser surgery on my eyes to correct for myopia—I didn't like wearing glasses and found contact lenses to be too bothersome. To my surprise, the doctor asked me if I wanted 20/20 vision or a bit better. Because I shoot targets with a pistol (for fun, not competitively), I opted for 20/20 vision in my left eye and a little better than that in my right, dominant eye. The result is that I can see the rear sight, the front sight, and the target more clearly at the same time, without shifting my focus to one and thereby blurring the other two. Having "normal" vision isn't optimal for all tasks, including target shooting.

Biomedical enhancements will keep coming in through the back door as long as we continue to make progress in treating diseases and disorders. So, just saying no to biomedical enhancements isn't really an option—unless we want to stop medical progress.

Yet if biomedical enhancements continue to come in through the back door, we'll have serious problems. Take Michelle's case. She and perhaps thousands of other students (and some professors) are taking a drug for a purpose for which it's not intended. There have been no clinical studies of the long-term use of Ritalin by people who don't have ADD. The worst-case scenario could be grim indeed. Ten years from now we discover that there's a serious adverse affect: People like Michelle develop some mental or physical problem. Ironically, some dimension of their cognitive performance gets worse; or they develop an emotional problem or personality disorder; or they suffer kidney or liver damage. So long as biomedical enhancements come through the back door, we won't be in a good position to evaluate their safety or even whether they really work for everybody who takes them.

The second issue the Michelle–Carlos dialogue raises is this: Just how novel are the problems biomedical enhancement raises? Michelle mentioned that cognitive enhancement drugs aren't new. We've had nicotine and caffeine for a long time. She also suggested that education is a cognitive enhancement technique. She could have gone further: Literacy is a fantastic cognitive enhancement. Being able to read and write greatly enhances what the human brain can do: Events and experiences can be recorded, and the record can be transmitted across vast distances and through the ages. We can make firm commitments in writing, avoiding some of the disagreements that would occur if we merely made oral pledges. We develop complex and enriching forms of discourse that wouldn't otherwise be possible. Each generation can build on the knowledge of previous ones, rather than having to start from scratch or depend on the vagaries of oral transmission.

Literacy and numeracy (mathematical skills) together have made possible perhaps the greatest cognitive enhancement to date: modern science. Computers and related technologies like smart phones are also awesome cognitive enhancements. They not only facilitate long-distance instantaneous communication, but also now include search engines like Bing, Google, and Yahoo that give us rapid access to vast amounts of information that we could never gain without them. Without computers the human genome couldn't have been sequenced and most medical research as we know it couldn't take place. Thanks to these nonbiomedical cognitive enhancements, human beings now have powers that our ancestors could only attribute to the gods.

These historical nonbiomedical cognitive enhancements don't just produce cognitive benefits. They produce wealthier societies; higher standards of living. They do this by making possible knowledge that can be applied to produce more food, better shelter, more goods, and more services. And the great institutional enhancement we call the market both stimulates the production of these good things and helps make them more widely available at lower cost.

Cognitive enhancements tend to increase productivity, and although increased productivity isn't to be confused with greater well-being, it tends to be a necessary condition for it. An unenhanced world is a miserably poor world with a tiny human population.

The problem is that in current discourse, the term "enhancement" is usually attached only to interventions that involve biomedical technologies. This blinds us to how pervasive enhancements are in our lives and how central they have been to the origin and evolution of our species. It also tempts us to assume—without really thinking it through—that there's something radically more problematic about biomedical enhancements than other enhancements.

Biomedical enhancements do present challenges; we'll be grappling with them throughout this book. But to keep those challenges in perspective, it's important to avoid *biomedical enhancement exceptionalism*—the dogmatic assumption that because an enhancement involves biotechnologies (pills, computers, fiddling with embryos, etc.) it's somehow off the moral scale, that our ordinary moral tool kit is useless for coping with it. As an antidote to biomedical exceptionalism it's important to remember that human history—or at least human progress—is in great part the story of enhancement.

Let me elaborate on this last point for a moment. I've already mentioned literacy, numeracy, science, and computers, but the list of enhancements that have played a crucial role in human progress is much longer than that. Think about what historians call the agrarian revolution, which occurred between eight and ten thousand years ago in the Middle East: the development of food crops along with the domestication of animals for plowing, transporting food, and as reliable sources of food, wool, and leather.

The first great effect of the agrarian revolution was that it enabled large numbers of people to live together year round. Before that, they lived in small, rather isolated groups and often had to move seasonally in search of food. Once large numbers of people could live together year round, they had to develop institutions—rule-governed patterns of behavior that greatly enhanced their capacities for social organization. We don't usually think of them in this way, but institutions are extraordinarily powerful enhancements.

The food surpluses the agrarian revolution produced made possible the division of labor; the development of commerce; leisure activities, and leisure goods and services ("luxuries"); the flourishing of arts and literature; and the development of government and with it the distinction between the public and the private sphere. The great nonbiomedical enhancements—institutions, literacy, numeracy, science—have made us who we are. You might even say they have shaped human nature.

Some people might protest that this isn't really progress. They pine for what they think of as the simplicity and harmony of an earlier kind of human life. For the past few decades, anthropologists have been chipping away at this idealized picture of the past—the notion that in premodern conditions human beings were peaceful, lived in harmony with nature, and were egalitarian. Those myths have now been shattered. In many scholarly articles and in books like *Sick Societies: Challenging the Myths of Primitive Harmony* by Robert Edgerton; *War Before Civilization: The Myth of the Peaceful Savage* by Lawrence H. Keeley; and *Collapse* by Jared Diamond, anthropologists have made a strong case that things weren't so good in the good old days. Some premodern societies committed suicide by ruining their environments; homicide rates among males in premodern societies were astronomically high; and the treatment of women (and often children as well) was frequently brutal. Unfortunately, the makers of the popular film *Avatar* were oblivious to these scientific findings. Those who doubt that the great historical enhancements have made human beings better off overall should ask themselves whether they would choose to have themselves—or their daughters—transported back to a hunting-gathering society.

Biomedical enhancements have provoked huge controversy. Given that enhancement isn't new and that it has played a central role in human progress, what's all the fuss? Why should we tie our hands, cut ourselves off from further progress, by forgoing enhancements just because they happen to use biomedical technologies? The answer must be that there is something radically different and profoundly more problematic about these enhancements because they are biomedical. What could that be?

Let's try some alternatives: (1) biomedical enhancements are different because they change our biology; (2) biomedical enhancements are different because (some of them) change the human gene pool; (3) biomedical enhancements are different because they could change or destroy human nature; (4) biomedical enhancements are different because they amount to playing God.

Playing God

Let's take the last one first. I once asked a scientist who inserts genes into mouse embryos if he was worried about the common allegation that people like him are playing God. His response was: "I'm not *playing*; I'm deadly serious!" That sort of reply doesn't inspire confidence, but fortunately, the attitude it expresses doesn't appear to be common among working scientists. And the scientist who made the remark laughed immediately afterward, indicating that what he said was tongue in cheek. The many scientists I've known have all been serious in the right way, and they don't come close to confusing themselves with the Deity.

The complaint about humans playing God isn't new, nor is it peculiar to biomedical enhancement. In the ancient Greek myth, Prometheus incurs the wrath of the gods because he gives fire to humans—the implication being that such a powerful technology is not suitable for mere mortals. The admonition not to play God is sometimes taken to be equivalent to "Don't interfere with nature." That's singularly unhelpful advice. As the philosopher John Stuart Mill pointed out 150 years ago, the term "nature" is ambiguous. It can mean the sum total of reality (including the laws of nature, for example, Force equals Mass times Acceleration). Or it can mean the way things would go without human action. In the first sense, the admonition not to interfere with nature isn't helpful, because we have no choice but to go along with nature. In the second sense, not interfering with nature would mean never acting and that, of course, isn't an option if we wish to live.

In the next two chapters we'll delve more deeply into whether the concept of nature or the natural can shed light on the ethics of biomedical enhancement. For now, the point I want to make is simply this: The slogan "Don't play God" is best understood as a warning against what the Greeks called hubris, over-weaning pride or being unjustifiably confident in our ability—in this case our ability to control our technologies.

That's good advice. But notice that it isn't just applicable to biomedical technologies; it applies to all technologies. Following this advice to be cautious *can't* mean never using any technologies. Refraining from using all technologies would betray either a desire for extinction or an unwarranted arrogant confidence that we can live without them. So, although it's of course true that we should avoid playing God if this just means "Don't be hubristic," it's not very helpful for making concrete, practical decisions about which technologies to use or how to use them.

The "Don't play God" slogan certainly doesn't enable us to draw a bright line between biomedical enhancements and other technologies, since it applies to both. It's simply a very general plea for caution: It can't tell us *how* to be cautious or when we are being too cautious or not cautious enough. It doesn't help us distinguish between arrogant folly and a reasonable optimism in attempting to improve our lot in life. "Don't play God" is at best a starting point for difficult thinking about how to balance risks and benefits, but unfortunately, many people invoke it as a substitute for thinking.

Changing the Human Gene Pool

The first thing to note here is that most biomedical enhancements wouldn't change the gene pool, because they don't involve changing genes. So, perhaps the concern is with one kind of biomedical enhancement: the genetic engineering of human embryos. In a trivial sense, any case of trying to improve an individual's capacities by inserting a gene into the embryo from which he develops would be changing the gene pool. That is, one individual would have a gene he wouldn't otherwise have. Whether that minor change would produce a significant effect in the gene pool—the totality of individual human genomes—would depend on whether the genetically altered individual had many offspring, whether many of them survived, and whether (and on what scale) they reproduced. Enhancement via genetic engineering would only be likely to have a significant effect on the human gene pool if either of two conditions were satisfied: Either a particular genetic alteration was undertaken on a very large scale, or an alteration undertaken on a small scale turned out to be highly beneficial in terms of reproductive fitness—that is, the gene spread through the human population over generations because having it greatly increased the chances of surviving and reproducing. In the latter case, altering the gene pool might be a good thing—for example, if the new gene protected us from emerging global pandemic diseases. So we shouldn't assume that changing the gene pool is always bad.

In 2001, the Council of Europe solemnly proclaimed that the human gene pool was the "common heritage" of mankind and therefore must be preserved. This declaration calls to mind the famous case of the ancient king of England, Canute, who commanded the waves of the ocean to cease. Talk about hubris.

The gene pool is changing all the time, through ordinary evolution, quite apart from deliberate human efforts to change it. Mutation of genes occurs randomly. Some mutations make it through the filter. So natural selection both presupposes and produces changes in the gene pool. The only way to preserve the human gene pool would be to store samples of everybody's genes and forbid any further reproduction.

The American bioethicist George Annas has gone the Council of Europe one better: He advocates changing international law to make genetic engineering of human embryos (for any reason, including enhancement) a "crime against humanity," to be prosecuted by the International Criminal Court. He too may be making the mistake of thinking that the gene pool is static unless altered by deliberate human intervention. At any rate, Annas is assuming not only that genetic enhancement would always be wrong, but that it would be so heinous as to warrant lumping it together with mass murder and genocide. What he is worried about, as it turns out, is that if some people are genetically enhanced and others aren't, the enhanced will prey on the unenhanced—that they will ruthlessly exploit or even exterminate them.

It's hard to know what to think about this grim prediction. I consider it in detail in chapter 5, but for now let's just say that it seems like a pretty speculative worry. More precisely, it looks like a crude "slippery slope" argument, the idea apparently being that allowing any genetic modification would be so likely to result in a two-class world of prey and predators that we are justified *now* in treating anybody who undertakes any genetic modification, no matter how minor or benign, like Slobodan Milosevic. International lawyers worry whether the new International Criminal Court will become credible and survive. If they thought anyone would take Annas's proposal seriously, they'd be a lot more worried.

Taken literally, warnings about genetic enhancements changing the gene pool don't make sense because the gene pool is always changing no matter what we do. Nevertheless, maybe, as with the case of the slogan "Don't play God," these warnings gesture rather clumsily toward something that is genuinely important. Perhaps the real worry is that deliberate efforts to change human genes will wreak havoc with the "natural" process by which evolution, operating through natural selection, alters the gene pool.

Notice that this way of understanding the warning about changing the gene pool assumes that evolution is doing a good job and that our efforts are likely to make things worse. That assumption, as I shall show in chapter 2, is an unsupported dogma. Ironically, although it claims to be an objection to genetic enhancement based on evolution, it's really the product of a pre-Darwinian understanding of nature as teleological—that is, the view that "natural" processes (so long as humans don't interfere with them) produce good results.

The father of evolutionary biology, Charles Darwin, thought otherwise. In a letter to his friend Joseph Hooker, he said so: "What a book a Devil's chaplain might write on the clumsy, wasteful, blundering, low, and horridly cruel works of nature!" Chapter 2 shows that this is not a cranky subjective judgment on Darwin's part: It's a characterization of nature that follows logically from an accurate understanding of evolution.

One last point about changing the gene pool. Only some biomedical enhancements necessarily involve changing the gene pool, namely, those that involve genetic engineering of human embryos or gametes (sperm or egg cells). But the great historical enhancements I described earlier have definitely changed the human gene pool in several ways. Here are four of them. First, the enhancement we call the agrarian revolution brought together large numbers of people in close proximity with each other and with animals such as pigs and chickens. This led to pathogens spreading not just from human to human but also from animals to humans (as with influenzas) and to epidemics. This changed the gene pool, because natural selection favored those who happened to have genes that conferred immunity to the diseases. Second, the great historical enhancements led to technologies and social institutions that facilitated migrations of peoples and long-distance commerce that brought previously isolated groups together. The result was that new combinations of genes occurred through old-fashioned, low-tech gene-splicing (i.e., sex). Third, the domestication of milk-producing animals led to selection of the genes associated with lactose tolerance. Because milk is a good source of fat and protein, being able to digest it confers an advantage in terms of reproductive fitness. But until some human societies developed the culture (no pun intended) of dairying, the gene that allowed infants to digest milk normally "switched off" as they became older. Fourth, the historical enhancements created new patterns of human interaction and new roles that may have significantly influenced sexual selection. Sexual selection, like natural selection, shapes the gene pool. It occurs in two ways: Males compete with each other for access to females (think of bucks sparring with their antlers during the mating season), and females gravitate to certain males because of characteristics they have. In birds, bright plumage signals freedom from parasites and, hence, general vigor. Or, according to another theory, it signals that the male is so vigorous that it can escape predation despite the handicap of being highly visible to predators.

Sexual selection of both types in humans is influenced by culture, and culture is profoundly influenced by the historical enhancements. The tendency of women to opt for males they think will be good providers may not have changed over the millennia. But the traits that contribute to being a good provider presumably have changed, as humans switched from hunting and gathering to agriculture and later to a complex economy based on the manipulation of digitalized information.

What's the relevance of all this? It means that if there is a difference between biomedical enhancements and other enhancements, it can't be that biomedical enhancements change the human gene pool. To repeat: Not all biomedical enhancements involve modifying genes—only genetic enhancements do and then only under certain conditions—and the most important nonbiomedical enhancements *have* changed the gene pool. More important, it is wrong just to *assume* that deliberately changing the gene pool would be a bad thing. Whether it would or wouldn't be depends on how good a job nature is doing in its ceaseless modification of the gene pool. That's the topic of the next chapter, but Darwin's grim assessment should at least give pause to those who think that natural is always best.

Changing Our Biology

Perhaps what makes biomedical enhancement so different—and especially problematic—is that it involves changing us physically or, more dramatically, that it alters our biology. Changing our biology certainly sounds like a big step, but what this would mean isn't so clear. Does drinking coffee change our biology? It does change our brain chemistry. If coffee doesn't change our biology, then why would one think that taking a cognitive enhancement drug in pill form would do so? What about genetic alteration of human embryos—would that count as changing our biology? That would depend on what sort of change was made. Some genetic changes might be fairly trivial, some might not be.

Oddly, human beings and only a few other mammalian species can't produce vitamin C from what they eat. In contrast, most mammals can "biosynthesize" this important chemical. The inability to biosynthesize vitamin C has caused huge problems for humans over the millennia. It still does for people who can't get enough vitamin C in their diet and can't afford or don't know about vitamin supplements. They get scurvy.

Humans can't make their own vitamin C because of a random mutation that occurred in our lineage about forty million years ago. So far as anyone can tell, there's no benefit that we gained from this change. Suppose that this could be corrected by genetic engineering—a paper has already been published explaining how it could be corrected in nonhuman animals. If that was the only change that was made, would it be helpful to say that human biology had been changed? Well, in one sense it would be, but in another, this would be hyperbolic, since everything else would remain the same. The right question to ask isn't whether it would change our biology, but whether it would be a good thing.

That old-fashioned cognitive enhancement, literacy, changes the structure of the brain. Strangely, there's evidence that being literate actually changes the visual center of the brain with the result that we perceive the human face differently than our preliterate ancestors did. In fact, learning anything, by any method, alters the brain by creating new connections among brain cells. Cognitive enhancement drugs, in contrast, only make transient changes that disappear when you stop taking the drug. Similarly, a brain-human interface technology that improved our thinking would only produce biological changes when it was being used.

Many potential biomedical enhancements—from taking enhancement drugs to minor genetic alterations to tissue implants to computer/human interface technologies—wouldn't alter our biology in any significant sense. But if they did, that's really not the question, unless we have good reason to think that changing our biology is always a bad idea. Our biology is a product of evolution. As such, it has changed in the past and will change in the future, regardless of whether we undertake biomedical enhancements. The question is whether we might have good reasons for deliberately changing our biology in some respects.

Now the very thought of changing our biology may be repugnant to some people because they assume that our biology is what is natural and that the natural is the good. The quote from Darwin already calls that assumption into question. I'll shine an even harsher, colder light on the assumption that natural is good in chapters 2 and 3. Here I want to begin to consider a related question: whether biomedical enhancements would change (or even destroy) *human nature* and, if so, whether that would be a bad thing. Answering that question will turn out to require a chapter, but for now we can at least begin to see why some people have thought it was the right question to ask about biomedical enhancements.

Changing or Destroying Human Nature

Francis Fukuyama, whose earlier book *The End of History* caused quite a stir for a time, wants a legal ban on genetic enhancement because it might inadvertently destroy that magical something that makes us human. I'll resist the temptation to say that, on the basis of his track record, we ought to be skeptical about Fukuyama's predictions. But it is perhaps worth mentioning that in his first book he wrongly predicted that the end of the Cold War would bring the end of ideology and hence of ideologically driven history. In doing so, he overlooked a few minor developments, including Islamic fundamentalism, the resurgence of socialism in parts of Latin America, and the clash between what some see as U.S. imperialism during the Bush administration and the commitment to the rule of international law, not to mention the rebirth of militaristic nationalism in post-Soviet Russia. Well, let's just set all that aside and consider his prediction about genetic enhancement on its own merits.

When people talk about human nature or what makes us human and in doing so assume that it is something precious that we ought not to imperil, they're taking a highly selective view of the subject. In fact, they are engaged in a whitewashing campaign of staggering proportions. After all, common sense and most major religions regard human nature as a pretty mixed bag. It includes awful as well as admirable features. In Christian terms, for example, although we are made in God's image, we are sinful by nature. As St. Paul puts it, we are "filthy rags"—a sanitized English translation of a Greek phrase more accurately rendered as "used toilet paper." Surely, Fukuyama would have to admit that human nature includes the bad as well as the good. So his real concern must be that if we undertake genetic enhancements, we will inadvertently destroy the good parts of our human nature.

Extreme Connectedness: Throwing Out the Baby with the Bathwater

If Darwin is right—if nature, or more accurately evolution, often makes a mess of things, including us, and if we could straighten some of this out by biomedical interventions— then perhaps we could improve human nature. Fukuyama and others who want a ban on genetic enhancement must be thinking that if we try to ameliorate the bad parts of human nature we will inadvertently destroy the good parts. Let's call this the Extreme Connectedness Assumption. What I find fascinating is that, although the Extreme Connectedness Assumption seems to lie at the heart of the fear and loathing of genetic enhancement that one finds in some quarters, no one acts like it's even worth thinking about, much less supporting with evidence.

What sort of evidence would be relevant? The answer is clear: scientific evidence about what evolved organisms like us are like. In other words, we have to look to biology. The great geneticist Theodosius Dobzhansky famously said that "nothing in biology makes sense except in the light of evolution." As the eminent philosopher of science Philip Kitcher notes, that might be a bit of an exaggeration. Yet this much is clear: Understanding evolution is critical for evaluating the Extreme Connectedness Assumption. And evaluating the Extreme Connectedness Assumption is critical for knowing how we ought to respond to the prospect of biomedical enhancement.

It shouldn't be surprising that in order to know whether in some instances genetic enhancement would be a good idea we need to know something about evolution. Yet those like Fukuyama and Annas who advocate a blanket prohibition on all genetic alteration of humans apparently don't agree. They think that from the smug comfort of their philosophical armchairs they can simply declare that all features of human nature are so closely interconnected that it would never be reasonable to try to ameliorate some of the worst features by altering genes. In chapter 2 I'll present a nontechnical but accurate account of some of the features of evolution that undermine the Extreme Connectedness Assumption. I'll argue that the baby and the bathwater can be separated.

Where We Stand So Far

My sense is that many people—perhaps the majority—are deeply concerned about the prospect of biomedical enhancements. The idea of trying to improve human beings by altering their genes— genetic enhancement—seems most worrisome of all. In fact, even the proposal to *consider* whether we should undertake genetic enhancements seems to elicit hysteria and loathing.

I haven't tried to argue for biomedical enhancements in general or for genetic enhancements in particular in this chapter. I'm just as leery of wild-eyed, Pollyanna-ish optimism about a "post-human future" as I am about knee-jerk, blanket rejections of biomedical enhancement. In my judgment, saying either that biomedical enhancements are an abomination or that they are wonderful would make about as much sense as being for or against technology or for or against globalization. Those generalizations are just too big to be useful. Even if in the end we conclude that genetic enhancements are not acceptable, we shouldn't tar all enhancements with the same brush. Different types and modes of biomedical enhancements deserve to be evaluated on their own account. We need to steer a steady course between hysterical loathing and breathless optimism.

In this chapter I've begun to correct for what I take to be an imbalance in the public perception of biomedical enhancement—a sort of unreflective, default negative attitude toward it. To try to correct this imbalance, I've done two things. First, I've shown that enhancement isn't new. On the contrary, human progress has depended on enhancement. Second, I've shown that we should be wary of biomedical enhancement exceptionalism—of unthinkingly assuming that because an enhancement involves biomedical means, it must somehow be especially profound in its effects or especially morally problematic. The great historical enhancements—the agrarian revolution, institutions, literacy, numeracy, and computers—have affected us profoundly; they've radically transformed human life and made us who we are. (In fact, it isn't at all obvious that biomedical enhancements will have so great an impact; many almost certainly won't.) Also, every one of the historical nonbiomedical enhancements has created moral challenges—in many cases the same ones that biomedical enhancement will create. Neither the problem of bad unintended consequences, nor the worry about worsening existing injustices is unique to *biomedical* enhancements. In fact, these problems arise for technologies generally, not just enhancement technologies.

All this only scratches the surface. In subsequent chapters I burrow deeper. Chapter 2 shows how the debate about the ethics of biomedical enhancement looks if we take evolution seriously. Chapter 3 explores the widely held assumption that reflecting on human nature can provide us with guidance in grappling with the ethical challenges of biomedical enhancement. Chapter 4 takes up the most serious worry about biomedical enhancement: the problem of unintended bad consequences. Chapter 5 probes the widely held belief that biomedical enhancements will exacerbate the problem of unfairness or distributive injustice. Chapter 6 examines a line of opposition to biomedical enhancement that is most closely identified with the work of Michael Sandel: the notion that the pursuit of enhancements both exhibits and contributes to vice—that is, bad character. The concluding chapter makes the case for embarking, cautiously and provisionally, on what I call the enhancement enterprise—meeting the challenge of biomedical enhancement head-on, rather than burying our heads in the sand and acting as if we can just say no.

2 | WHY EVOLUTION ISN'T GOOD ENOUGH

Nature red in tooth and claw...

ALFRED LORD TENNYSON

The poet Tennyson says nature is bloody. Darwin, in the letter to Hooker quoted in chapter 1, says it is bloody *and inept* ("clumsy" and "blundering"). Tennyson was no doubt an astute observer of the mayhem that seethes beneath the pastoral surface of rural life in England (or anywhere else, for that matter): creatures great and small ripping each other apart, devouring each other alive, day in, day out. Darwin was a scientist, not a poet. His assessment of nature is more systematic and more solidly grounded. Darwin had a theory—what turned out to be the best theory—of just why nature is both bloody and inept.

How you think about nature will profoundly shape your attitude toward biomedical enhancement in general, but especially *genetic* enhancements. Some of the harshest critics of genetic enhancements, including G.W. Bush's President's Council on Bioethics, have a view of nature that makes any attempt at genetic enhancement look like a harebrained, ultra-risky endeavor. They think that genetic enhancement is going against the wisdom of nature.

The Bush Council *says* that their view of nature is scientific—that it is grounded in an understanding of evolution. So they extol the wisdom of nature in evolutionary terms. Consider the following passage from *Beyond Therapy*, the Council's book on enhancement.

The human mind and body, highly complex and delicately balanced as the result of eons of exacting evolution, are almost certainly at risk from any ill-considered attempt at "improvement." . . . It is far from clear that our delicately integrated natural bodily powers will take kindly to such impositions, however desirable the sought-for change may seem to the intervener.

Let's set aside the prejudicial rhetoric about "imposition." (An imposition is a burdensome or improper intervention; that's prejudicial, because we are supposed to be determining whether genetic enhancements *are* improper interventions, not simply assuming they are.) The first thing to notice is that the quoted passage presents in evolutionary guise a common objection to biomedical enhancement—the idea that it is foolish to interfere with the wisdom of nature. The President's Council isn't alone: The highly respected philosophers Nick Bostrom and Anders Sandberg, who also approach genetic enhancement from an evolutionary standpoint, warn that when "an over-ambitious tinkerer with merely superficial understanding of what he is doing [makes] changes to the design of a master engineer, the potential for damage is considerable and the chances of making an all-things-considered improvement are small." The quote from Bostrom and Sandberg makes explicit something implied by the Council's talk about "eons of exacting evolution" and the organism being "finely balanced" and "delicately integrated": the idea that *evolution is like a master engineer*.

If evolution is like a master engineer, then organisms are like engineering masterpieces: beautifully designed, harmonious, finished products that are stable and durable (if we leave them alone). If that's what we are like, then biomedical enhancement is reckless indeed. Genetic enhancement—seen as an attempt to change the master design itself—seems especially ill-conceived. The master engineer analogy, if it is accurate, provides a strong argument against genetic enhancement and perhaps against biomedical enhancement generally.

There's something odd about the master engineer analogy. It smacks of pre-Darwinian religious thought about the created world—the previously dead and buried, but recently resurrected argument from intelligent design. The only difference is that the evolutionary version of the master engineer analogy substitutes natural selection for God's creative genius.

The resemblance between the religious argument from intelligent design and the appeal to evolution as a master engineer is disturbing, because the Darwinian revolution was supposed to have overthrown the argument from intelligent design. After all, Darwin's big point was that nature *doesn't* exhibit *intelligent* design. According to Darwinian theory, natural selection solves problems organisms face by redesigning the organism, but it doesn't do so the way a master engineer would. The designing that evolution accomplishes through natural selection isn't just nonconscious; it's downright unintelligent. What evolution produces is not beautifully designed, harmonious, completed masterworks that will endure so long as we don't meddle with them. Instead, it produces cobbled-together, unstable works in progress, and then discards them.

Organisms are remarkably unlike the work of a master engineer in two fundamental respects. First, unlike a master engineer, natural selection never gets the job done: Existing organisms, including human beings, are not the end points of a process whereby they climb the ladder to perfect adaptation to their environment. The environment is always changing, in part due to the fact that organisms compete with one another in a ceaseless round of adaptation and counteradaptation. One example is pathogens such as flu viruses. They're constantly changing to overcome our changing defenses against them. It's a relentless arms race: We develop resistance to one virus strain, and then natural selection produces another one that we don't have resistance to and so on. There's no constant environment to which our species is getting better and better adapted. In the case of human beings, there's another source of change: We've become so powerful that we keep changing our environment, sometimes producing new problems (like global warming), which we then have to adapt to. The idea that the evolved organism is "finely balanced" implies a stability that simply doesn't exist.

Second, unlike a master engineer, evolution doesn't design what it produces according to a plan that it draws up in advance. Instead, it modifies organisms in response to *short-term* problems, with no thought of long-term effects. Evolution has no overall game plan for any species, and the results show it. What's useful for solving today's problem can cause new problems—and even extinction—down the line.

To summarize: The master engineer analogy claims to take Darwinian evolution seriously, but it's just the old pre-Darwinian view of the wisdom of nature thinly disguised. It simply misses the point of Darwin's revolution in biology.

In the rest of this chapter, I want to say enough about what evolution is like to convince you to toss out the master engineer analogy and embrace a much less consoling one. I want to show that evolution is more like a *morally blind, fickle, tightly shackled tinkerer*. Making the case for this metaphor will require a little patience on your part. We'll have to master some relevant features of evolution. But there's no way to get around it. How we think about evolution—or, if you prefer, nature—makes all the difference to how we *should* think about enhancement. Interfering with the work of a master engineer is one thing; selectively intervening in the work of a morally blind, fickle, tightly shackled tinkerer is quite another.

Suboptimal Design: It's Everywhere

It's ironic that proponents of the master engineer analogy invoke natural selection, because it's the *imperfection* of biological design that led Darwin to the theory of natural selection in the first place. Darwin debunked the argument from *intelligent* design, one of the traditional arguments for the existence of God, by cataloguing the "clumsy, wasteful, blundering" works of nature. Here's just a small sample of the sort of design flaws that spurred Darwin to develop the theory of natural selection.

1. The urinary tract in male mammals passes through (rather than being routed around) the prostate gland, which can swell and block urinary function
2. Poor drainage in the primate sinuses, which can lead to severe pain and infection
3. The inability of anthropoid primates (including humans) to bio-synthesize vitamin C, which has led to countless deaths from scurvy
4. The "blind spot" in the eyes of vertebrates, which results from quirks of embryological development and which required verte-brates to develop elaborate and costly perception-correcting mechanisms
5. The dual function of the human pharynx—air intake and food intake—which significantly increases the chance of death by choking, compared to other animals
6. The hasty shift from quadruped to biped, which resulted in back and knee problems and a birth canal that passes through the pelvis, resulting in greatly increased risks to both mother and child in the birthing process

Design flaws are found in all species. For example, bats spend a good deal of their time hanging upside down, closely packed together, with their feces pouring down over their bodies to their heads. (Imagine yourself holding a toothpaste tube upright and squeezing it until the contents cover your hands. That's what it's like to be a bat.) The result is not just disgusting; it's dangerous, because it promotes infectious diseases.

The Mechanisms of Evolution

Once we consider how evolution works, the pervasiveness of design flaws will come as no surprise. They aren't exceptions—the occasional results of Mother Nature having a bad day. They're perfectly predictable results.

In a recent scholarly article, the brilliant young philosopher of biology Russell Powell and I use a comparison between unintentional genetic modification (UGM) and intentional genetic modification (IGM) to help explain just why evolution is *not* like a master engineer.

UGM is evolution as usual, what Darwin called "descent with modification," where a driving force of the modification is natural selection. UGM, in other words, is evolution without intentional modification of human genes by human beings. IGM is intentional genetic modification.

Powell and I compare UGM and IGM *as regards their respective potentials for improving—or even sustaining—human life.* To make the comparison, we first describe the quite severe *limitations* on UGM as a mechanism for improving or sustaining human life and then show how IGM could overcome each of these limitations. In effect, we ask: If you could choose (and we *can* choose), which would you entrust human well-being to—UGM or UGM supplemented selectively with IGM? Here I'll just summarize our argument, avoiding technical jargon as best I can.

UGM's Insensitivity to Post-reproduction Quality of Life

Mother Nature neglects her elderly children. Natural selection works as a gene filter: It tends to prevent genes that have a greater negative impact *on reproductive fitness* than other genes from being passed on to the next generation. A gene increases reproductive fitness if having it contributes to a trait that increases the chances that the organism that has that trait will successfully reproduce. Once the organism is beyond reproductive age, there's little if any filtering: Traits that undermine the elderly's quality of life don't get winnowed out. (Some evolutionary biologists think that there are some minor exceptions to this, but most agree that there's little hope for natural selection weeding out the vast majority of things that go wrong as we get older.)

This explains a lot. Old humans typically suffer a number of problems that would seriously compromise reproductive fitness in younger individuals: decreased libido, osteoarthritis, much higher rates of cancer and cardiovascular disease, and neural degeneration resulting in compromised cognitive performance and eventually dementia (30% of people over 85 and 50% of people over 90 get Alzheimer's, and that isn't counting dementia that results from strokes). The fact that natural selection doesn't operate in the post-reproductive period of our lives is a sharp blow against the master engineer analogy. What kind of master engineer creates beings that begin to fall apart once they've passed reproductive age and makes no provision for repair?

Many people—perhaps most—assume that according to Darwin's account of evolution all biological traits are either the direct result of natural selection or a side effect of it. That's incorrect: The vast majority of post-reproductive traits are neither. Once our reproductive years are over, there's no "investment" in mechanisms to repair the damage that afflicts the elderly. This unfortunate fact about the way evolution works has especially dire consequences for long-lived organisms like us.

If we weren't lulled into thinking that "that's just how it is when you get older" we'd think that a person who exhibited these symptoms had some ghastly disease! But perhaps it doesn't have to continue to be the way it has always been. One of the chief advantages of IGM (intentional genetic modification) is that it could help us avoid or ameliorate the harms we suffer as a result of UGM's insensitivity to post-reproductive quality of life. For example, modifications of tumor-causing genes (switching them off completely or at least making them less likely to cause cancer) and of tumor-suppressing genes (strengthening their protective power) could counteract the tendency of accumulated mutations to cause cancer later in life. Intervening in the genetic networks that regulate hormones could prevent or retard muscle loss and debilitating frailty in the elderly. These are only two examples of the potential for IGM to correct for one of the greatest flaws of UGM.

Our post-reproductive quality of life matters more and more because we are living much longer (average life expectancy for males in the United States in 1900 was 47 years). We live longer due to the cumulative impact of the great historical nonbiological enhancements. We may need further enhancements—including biomedical ones—to cope with the consequences of these earlier enhancements.

When we make a judgment that a person had a good life, we tend to take into account the quality of that life overall, over its entire span. If people were routinely living to be 110, but had a very poor quality of life for the last 25 years, this would affect our judgments about the quality of their lives. We might well conclude that most people lived better lives when people didn't live so long but had a shorter period of declining quality of life. If that is so, then biomedical enhancements that enable us to live a very long life, with the worst ailments compressed into a very short period at the end, might be needed just to sustain the present average level of well-being in our lives. In other words, paradoxically, *we may need to enhance, just to keep things from getting worse*. This turns out to be a pretty important point: It shows that people like Michael Sandel, who say that enhancement is the quest for perfection, or those like Carl Elliot, who say that it is an attempt to be better than well, are wrong. The fact that enhancement may be needed to prevent things from getting worse turns out to make a world of difference as to how we should think about enhancement, as we'll see in a later chapter.

Pleistocene Hangovers

The master engineer analogy may seem apt if you think that every trait an organism has is an adaptation. We've already seen that that's not true: There's nothing adaptive about the traits that undermine the quality of life in old age; they aren't the product of natural selection. And even when a trait is an adaptation, it is not likely to be the best of all possible adaptations.

It's worth focusing more closely on what adaptation is. The statement "Trait T is an adaptation" is framed in the present tense, but it's really a statement about the past. It means that at some earlier point in the development of the species, organisms having that trait increased their chances of passing on their genes to the next generation. In other words, identifying something as an adaptation says something about where it came from; it says nothing about what it does now! Yesterday's advantage may be today's liability, so the fact that a trait is an adaptation doesn't mean it's a good thing.

Evolutionary biologists think that most of the biological traits you and I have are the result of selective pressures during the late Pleistocene Era, around 100,000 or 150,000 years ago. There have been changes since then—for example, epidemics have swept through human populations resulting in some genes being extinguished and others (the ones that confer resistance) spreading more widely. But the basic biological features have pretty much remained the same.

During the period when our basic biology was being shaped, the environment was radically different from what it is today. Humans lived in small hunter-gatherer bands, not in teeming cities doing increasingly sedentary work using information technologies. Because the environment we live in now is so different, some of the traits we have that are adaptations (remember, that's a backward-looking statement) may be maladaptive today. Here are some likely examples. (1) The predilection for sweet, salty, and fatty foods. Having this trait is great, if you are a hunter-gatherer who has to invest a lot of time and energy to feed yourself. If you work at a desk all day and can gratify your taste buds almost instantaneously anytime the urge strikes, it's not so good: The result may be obesity, diabetes, and coronary artery disease. (2) The tendency of stepfathers to abuse their stepchildren (more than their own children). From the standpoint of what Richard Dawkins calls the "selfish gene," this shameful behavior makes perfectly good sense: Why would one expect an organism, hovering on the edge of subsistence a hundred thousand years ago, to waste resources on sustaining some other guy's gene line? If there's competition for survival within the species, one would expect not only neglect but abuse, and unfortunately that's what we sometimes see. (3) Nastiness toward "foreigners," the lamentably widespread tendency to fear strangers (xenophobia) or at least to be indifferent to their welfare. This trait may have been conducive to survival and reproduction in the Pleistocene, but in an increasingly globalized world in which human beings have to interact with strangers—and where weapons of mass destruction are available not only to countries but to small groups or even a single individual—it may prove disastrous. (4) There's speculation that attention deficit disorder, which occurs disproportionately in males, is yet another example. It might have been a good thing in the Pleistocene for males, if they did most of the hunting, to be acutely aware of what was going on in their peripheral vision and constantly shifting their focus from here to there. But when you're expected to spend most of your day sitting at a desk, looking at a textbook or a blackboard or a computer screen, this causes problems.

Evolutionary hangovers aren't confined to *Homo sapiens. Canis familiaris* (your dog) may suffer from them as well. It's hardly surprising that some of the traits that were valuable for your golden retriever's distant ancestors cause problems when he spends most of his time indoors, bereft of the fellowship of the pack.

It would be a mistake to assume that evolution will eventually extinguish such hangovers. They can cause serious problems for those of us who have them without reducing our reproductive fitness disastrously enough to get winnowed out. In other words, the mesh of the filter may not be fine enough to stop the genes responsible for them from being passed on and on. And even when they do have a negative impact on reproductive fitness, the evolutionary cure may be excruciatingly slow—taking many thousands of years. In principle, IGM could clean up the unwanted residue from our ancient past much more quickly and effectively. Less radically, drugs could be used to counteract the effects of Pleistocene hangover genes. Perhaps that's what Ritalin does.

How Beneficial Mutations Spread: A Nasty, Brutish, and Long Process

So far we've considered how deficient UGM is from the standpoint of getting rid of bad traits. There's also a big problem with how it creates good traits. It can take thousands of years and untold human misery for a new beneficial trait to spread throughout the population. For example, our ancestors had to suffer enormously high death rates from diseases like smallpox and bubonic plague before genes that confer resistance to these diseases could become relatively widespread. In addition, the beneficial change often comes at a steep price for some people. This is the case with the mutation associated with sickle cell trait. If you have one copy of the gene you get resistance to malaria; if you have two copies you get that plus a high likelihood that you'll have sickle cell anemia, a debilitating disease.

It's often thought that Darwin's big impact on religion was that his theory of natural selection exploded the argument that the intelligent design we see in nature presupposes a divine creator. But once we contemplate the nasty, brutish, and long process by which beneficial genes spread through populations, we may conclude that his theory strikes another equally devastating blow against religion: It shows that the Problem of Evil is even worse than we thought.

The Problem of Evil is this: Given how much human suffering there is in the world—much of it utterly undeserved—how could such a world be the creation of a being that is both all-powerful and supremely good? Francis Collins, former director of the National

Human Genome Project and current director of the National Institutes of Health, appears to overlook the implications of Darwin's theory for the Problem of Evil when he tries to show how a scientist like himself can consistently believe in God. Collins thinks it's pleasantly amazing that God chose to use evolution to create the living world, because evolutionary theory has a stunningly elegant simplicity. Collins seems to think it's more creative—or at least more aesthetically pleasing to the mind of the scientist—for God to use evolution than simply to snap his fingers and have the world appear.

The obvious question to ask is this: If God is supremely good, why would he choose such a bloody mode of creation? Recall how this chapter began—with one quote from Tennyson about nature being red in tooth and claw and a reminder of Darwin's description of nature as horridly cruel. God can do anything. If He chose evolution as the mechanism of life because it was the most elegant, in spite of the fact that it is so awfully bloody, how could He be supremely good? It's not just that the propagation of desirable genes is usually a grisly process; the whole survival of the fittest thing is astonishingly cruel. Because Collins focuses on the elegant simplicity of evolution and downplays the gore, his scientist's case for God is less than convincing.

Collins is aware of the Problem of Evil, however. He thinks that our suffering is compatible with God's goodness because suffering enriches our lives, builds character, etc. That old chestnut isn't very satisfying for two reasons. First, many humans—especially children who die from violence or diseases and the millions of young men who die in war—experience suffering without much opportunity for gaining from it. God's making *them* suffer so that *you and I* can have a deeper appreciation of existence seems obscenely unfair. Second, it appears there's *surplus* suffering: God seems to have given us more than enough of it to make his point.

Suppose for a moment that in spite of these obvious difficulties, we accept the notion that our lives are enriched by suffering—so wonderfully enriched as to make it worthwhile for us. That's hardly relevant to the massive suffering of the rest of creation. The elk that's devoured by wolves while still alive can't console itself with the thought that elk life is enriched by character-building suffering. Thinking that the good that humans get from *our* suffering is so wonderful that we can simply turn a blind eye to the misery of all the other creatures seems a tad anthropocentric to me. The Buddha felt the same way: He appreciated that all living things suffer. That's one of the most admirable aspects of Buddhism and one from which other religions could learn a great deal. I don't know whether Buddhism is especially attractive to people who understand how evolution works, but perhaps it should be.

The central point is that IGM has the potential to achieve the good results of UGM, without the butcher's bill. For example, suppose we learn that some desirable gene or set of genes already exists, but only in a small number of humans. This is precisely the situation for genes that confer resistance to certain strains of HIV-AIDS. If we rely on the "wisdom of nature" or "let nature take its course," this beneficial genotype may or may not spread through the human population. The small group of humans in which it exists might die in a natural catastrophe or a war, or those who have it might happen to have some other, less beneficial genes that reduce their reproductive fitness. Even if the desirable genes do spread, it will take a very long time—probably thousands of years. In the meantime, millions will suffer and die. It would take a lot of elegance to make up for this sort of thing.

Suppose it were possible to ensure that such beneficial genes spread much more quickly by IGM. This could occur by injecting genes into the testicles or, more radically, by inserting them into a large number of human embryos, utilizing IVF (in vitro fertilization). We would get the benefits of IGM when it operates optimally, without the carnage.

To summarize: Evolution doesn't count the costs of its improvements and it doesn't care how the costs are distributed—it's morally blind. If IGM can achieve the good that UGM achieves and do so not only more quickly, but also without the moral costs, then that counts heavily in favor of it.

The Improbability of "Lateral" Gene Transfer

You and I and other animals can do a lot of things that bacteria can't. But they've got a couple of items in their evolutionary bag of tricks that we lack. One of their most dazzling tricks is that they regularly incorporate new genes without inheriting them—they have lateral gene transfer. Genes are transmitted vertically when they are passed on from one generation to the next, through sexual reproduction. If you're an animal, for the most part the only genes you have access to are those your parents had. It's true that sometimes viruses become part of the human genome and they can bring new genes with them that we didn't inherit through regular human reproduction. But this is pretty rare.

In contrast, if you're a bacterium, and there's a beneficial gene in the neighborhood, you can grab it. Lateral gene transfer greatly increase genetic resources.

Bacteria have another big advantage: The time it takes them to reproduce is incredibly short compared to ours. The combination of these two features—lateral gene transfer and a short reproductive cycle—gives them a huge advantage in the human-pathogen arms race. It's hard for us to keep up with the rapidity and flexibility of mutation in these critters. That's why we produce new flu vaccines almost every year but still remain vulnerable to unpredicted novel strains.

IGM, unlike UGM in animals, is not limited to vertical gene transfer. Scientists already know how to take genes from one mouse lineage and insert them into other, unrelated mice, and they can do this for many animals. IGM isn't even limited to borrowing genes from conspecifics—organisms of the same species. Scientists routinely insert human genes into mice to do research on diseases that affect humans.

Switching genes from one organism to another works, for two reasons. First, all life has the same biochemical basis, using the same four nucleic acid base pairs that form the steps of the ladderlike structure of DNA. Second, all current living things descended from a common ancestor, and the majority of ancestral genes are conserved over the eons. For example, humans and mice have 80% *identical* genes, and up to 99% of human genes have mouse counterpart genes.

When genetic engineering was first invented, some people warned that using genes from other species will "breach species barriers"—and implied that this would be very dangerous.

Talk about species barriers is evocative, but it's unclear how apt it is. Given how many genes we have in common with other species and given that species aren't rigidly fixed, but constantly evolving, it's doubtful whether the idea of species barriers even makes sense. (For what it's worth, my great uncle broke down "species barriers" for a living, apparently without ill effect: He bred mules.)

Because UGM, unassisted evolution, can rely only on vertical gene transfer, it's like a workman shackled to a bench in one corner of a vast warehouse brimming with valuable materials. With IGM, the workman can throw off his shackles and pick and choose what he needs.

The Danger of Losing Valuable Genes Forever

A few years ago a universal seed depository, burrowed deep into a mountain in Norway, opened for business. Its purpose is to provide secure storage for as many different types of plant seeds as possible. It could just as well be described as a gene bank, since each seed contains the complete complement of genes needed to make a plant. This facility is a prudent hedge against loss of genetic diversity in plants, which is presently occurring at an alarming rate and which might greatly accelerate if there were a "nuclear winter" or some massive natural disaster.

When species go extinct, their unique genes are usually lost forever. In fact, as we saw earlier, even when natural selection doesn't result in species extinction, it *reduces* genetic variation, by serving as a gene filter. That's an unfortunate fact about UGM, because some genes that are irrevocably lost may be of great value for improving human life or even for preserving it in the face of new threats, whether natural or man-made.

IGM, when combined with prudent preservation, can avoid the irrevocable loss of valuable genes. This is an important point and an ironic one, in the light of a common complaint about IGM, namely, that it will *decrease* genetic diversity. Those who make this complaint worry that we will use IGM to indulge in the folly of "monoculture," creating a standard type of new human, with a specific genotype, and allowing all other human genotypes to go extinct. The problem of monoculture is well known to horticulturists. For example, in the 1890s, elm trees were planted all over Minneapolis-St. Paul. Fifty years later almost all of them were dead of Dutch elm disease.

The risk of monoculture is not to be dismissed, but it has to be put in perspective. First, we need to appreciate the fact that UGM, because it relies on the gene filter of natural selection, reduces genetic diversity as a matter of course and that this has its risks. Second, we need to understand that IGM may be the only effective way to *counter* the risks of decreased genetic diversity. There are already several hundred million stored human tissue samples in the United States alone. Each has a complete human genotype (so long as there is one cell with one intact nucleus). More and more tissue samples—all of which are genotype samples—are being collected every day, mainly in the context of drug research. IGM makes it possible to draw on this huge genetic bounty, to reintroduce valuable genes that are in danger of going extinct in the normal course of UGM or, as we saw earlier, to speed up the proliferation of valuable genes.

I became much less concerned that humanity would somehow agree on a standard model of *Homo sapiens* and thereby create its own monoculture problem when I witnessed an exchange between two students in my Ethical Issues in Genetics class. A rather Nordic-looking student said, "Yeah, I suppose it could be a problem—parents might all decide they wanted to have tall, blond kids with blue eyes." A student from Nigeria sitting next to him quickly replied, "I don't think so." The Nigerian lad had a point: There may not be as much consensus on what's the best kind of human as the prophets of human monoculture suppose. The big point, however, is that if we value genetic diversity, we should worry more about UGM and less about IGM.

Local Optimality Traps, or You Can't Get There from Here

From the standpoint of evolution, to say that a trait is optimal means that no further *incremental* changes in the organism's genes can improve the trait's contribution to reproductive fitness.

Optimal doesn't mean unimprovable. It only means "the best that can be done, from the standpoint of reproductive fitness, *given that this is where we are now and that we have to proceed incrementally*." Suppose the trait is a complex one, like vision. Human beings have a particular kind of visual apparatus: A camera-like eye that has a blind spot and that requires the brain to sort out the upside-down images it creates. There are other types of eyes in other species and there are some possible types of eyes that never evolved. The fact that we have the kind of eyes we do doesn't mean that they are optimal in the sense of being the best eyes for human beings to have, much less the best eyes period.

The human eye developed through a long process of incremental changes, starting eons ago with a mutation or series of mutations that produced a light-sensitive patch on the surface of a critter that wasn't much like us. The light-sensitive patch gave the critter a survival edge because it enabled it to detect movements of objects around it. Similarly, there's a possible series of biological changes that could lead from the human eye as it is now to a different type of eye, one that would be better for us as a visual apparatus.

Using only the mechanism of natural selection, the transformation of our existing eye to a superior type would require a staggeringly large number of changes and an almost imponderable length of time. It might never occur, because we might be trapped in what evolutionary biologists call a local optimality.

The idea of a local optimality trap is best explained with an analogy. Consider a "fitness landscape" represented in three dimensions. Under the pressures of natural selection, a species climbs a fitness peak. Fitness peaks are of varying heights, where height represents reproductive fitness: the higher the peak, the more conducive to reproductive fitness a particular set of traits is. Imagine that you and I and all other humans have scaled a fitness peak that has an elevation of 2,000 meters. We're a lot better off, in terms of reproductive fitness, than if we were only atop a 1,000-meter peak. But we can look out across the valley and see a much higher peak. The problem is that to get to the higher peak, we would have to take a long journey, step by step, that would take us across a deep valley and then up the slopes of the higher peak. In other words, we would have to lose ground in terms of fitness, relative to where we presently are, in order to get to greater fitness. We're trapped in a local optimality: We can't increase our reproductive fitness, not because there are no biologically possible changes that would improve it, but because we can't get there from here. Because natural selection is incremental, it can't leap over the valleys to reach the higher peaks.

In principle, IGM could solve this problem, because it could produce nonincremental changes by making them very early on in our development, through modifying the genes of embryos. I mentioned earlier that evolution is like a *tightly shackled* tinkerer, at least when it comes to animals as opposed to bacteria, because it can usually only utilize genes that happen to exist in the lineage of a particular organism. It can only rarely borrow genes laterally. The phenomenon of local optimality traps shows that the tinkerer is tightly shackled in another way: Because he works only incrementally, some improvements that are of enormous potential value are forever beyond his reach.

The Biggest Limitation: UGM Selects for Reproductive Fitness, Not Human Good

The term "optimality" causes a lot of confusion in the context of discussions about evolution. In evolutionary theory, optimal doesn't mean best; it means most conducive to reproductive fitness. To say that a trait increases reproductive fitness is just to say that having it increases an organism's chances of passing on its genes to its descendants.

The first thing to note, as we've already seen, is that the fact that a trait exists doesn't mean that it contributes to reproductive fitness. It may exist because it tags along with some trait that does contribute to reproductive fitness. Or it may exist because it occurs after reproduction and isn't subject to the filter of natural selection. Or it may have contributed to reproductive fitness in earlier generations, but now is either neutral or a detriment to reproductive fitness. So, we shouldn't make the mistake of thinking that because we have a trait, it must be doing some good, from the standpoint of reproductive fitness. There's a bigger mistake—one with much greater potential for confusing the enhancement debate: the error of equating "conducive to reproductive fitness" with "good."

If what we cared about was maximizing the number of human genes passed on to future generations, then one way to do this might be to increase the human population up to the Malthusian breaking point—that is, for everybody to have as many children as possible, even if this meant that everybody merely subsisted, living in dire poverty, deprived of most of what makes for a *good* human life.

The big point is that reproductive fitness is about quantity, not quality. That's why it's a gross blunder to think that when a trait contributes to reproductive fitness, it's good and that changing it wouldn't be an improvement. If we're reproducing well enough to replace ourselves, or at least to maintain the minimum population needed to sustain the progress we've already made over the centuries by enhancing ourselves, what matters is the kind of life we live, not the quantity of human genes in the future.

With this crucial distinction between reproductive fitness and human good in mind, we can now ask an important question: In what sense, if any, is the existing version of humanity *optimal*? If we answer this question on the basis of an accurate understanding of evolution, here's what we *can't* say. We can't say that current humans are the best, if this means best in terms of what we rightly value. The fact that we are what evolution has produced so far doesn't tell us anything about how good we are when it comes to what really matters, because evolution isn't about producing what's valuable.

In fact, we can't even say that we are best in terms of reproductive fitness; all we can say is that we are doing well enough that the human population is increasing, not decreasing. We can't even say that we are optimal from the standpoint of reproductive fitness, because natural selection doesn't typically maximize reproductive fitness, it merely approximates it, and then only fleetingly. Nor can we say that we are the best in the sense of being better adapted to our environment than earlier versions of humanity or our prehuman ancestors. That makes no sense, because adaptation is always relative to an environment and our environment is radically different from that of our ancestors. Shocking as this may sound, we can't even say that we are more likely to survive as a species longer than Neanderthals or dinosaurs, or any other species that preceded us on this planet. In fact, even if humans had already existed longer than the oldest species that ever lived, that wouldn't show that we are better adapted in the sense of having greater prospects for continued survival. In more technical evolutionary terms, the age of a biological lineage is *not* correlated with its current prospects of survival. That makes perfectly good sense, once we understand that adaptive success is always relative to a particular environment and that "the" environment is always changing. For all these reasons, we have to steadfastly resist the common tendency to think that the latest product of the evolutionary process is the best, either biologically speaking, or in terms of human values. We can't say we are the best in either sense, and that's why we should take the possibility of biomedical enhancement seriously.

In my youth, what passed for world history textbooks typically had a page or two on evolution, with a drawing of "the Ascent of Man." It consisted of a series of figures from left to right, beginning with a fish-like critter hauling itself out of the primordial slime, followed by an odd-looking mammal on all fours, followed by a knuckle-walking ape, followed by a Neanderthal with poor posture dressed in skins, and ending, on the far right, with a white guy in a business suit, standing perfectly erect. The idea was that the latest is the best and that evolution is over now that we've arrived. I suspect that a lot of us who now laugh at that picture still hang onto the thoroughly un-Darwinian assumptions it expresses.

Analogy Wars

How we think about evolution or nature makes a big difference as to how we think about biomedical enhancement. If evolution is like a master engineer, then trying to improve existing capacities by biomedical means is hubristic and risky. We'd better stick with "the wisdom of nature." But if evolution is more like a morally blind, fickle, tightly shackled tinkerer, then nature isn't so wise and there's lots of room for improvement.

This analogy is even less flattering than a famous analogy drawn by the eminent evolutionary biologist Richard Dawkins. He says that evolution—more specifically, natural selection—is like a blind watchmaker. In fact, Dawkins's analogy is too charitable. A blind watchmaker begins with a plan and he aims to satisfy a human need. Evolution does neither.

My complex characterization of the tinkerer isn't just rhetoric. Every adjective is apt, given the limitations of evolution I've outlined in this chapter. Evolution is morally blind in two senses: It's not about human improvement or even human well-being, and when it does happen to achieve what's good for us the means it uses are typically ghastly. It's fickle, in that it shapes species and then discards them. The only reliable prediction about evolution we can make is that all species go extinct eventually. It's tightly shackled in two senses: For anything beyond bacteria, lateral gene transfer is extremely infrequent, so mountains of desirable genes aren't available to unassisted evolution; and because natural selection produces change incrementally and at best only achieves "local" optimality, there are lots of potential improvements, higher "fitness peaks," it can't get to.

If we swallow the master engineer analogy, biomedical enhancement looks pretty dubious, and genetic enhancement looks especially misguided. I've exposed the flaws of the master engineer analogy. I've also shown that from the standpoint of improving or even preserving human well-being, intentional genetic modification has significant advantages over unintentional genetic modification, evolution as usual.

A House of Cards?

All right; so evolution isn't a master engineer and organisms aren't masterpieces of engineering. Maybe that makes biomedical enhancements even more dangerous! If we were the products of a master engineer, we might be able to figure out how we work and even how we could be improved, because we'd be constructed in a rational, intelligent way. On the other hand, if we are jerry-rigged Rube Goldberg contraptions, slapped together by a morally blind, fickle, insensitive tinkerer, we may be much harder to figure out. So maybe the right analogy is a house of cards: Given how poorly designed we are, we are likely to be fragile. But if we're fragile, all the more reason not to try to intervene in our biology.

This anti-enhancement argument has the virtue of originality, but that's about all it has going for it. If we're so poorly designed as to be extremely fragile, then we may need improvement if we are to survive. More specifically, we need to be modified so that we aren't so fragile. Remember, the environment is changing, so if we are like a house of cards, we aren't likely to survive for long. If we are "finely balanced," not in a stable, well-thought-out way, but in the way a house of cards is, this seems to be an intolerable situation. Why think that it is only our efforts at biomedical enhancement that are likely to cause the house of cards to collapse? A small change in the environment might do it. We may have already changed our environment in ways that will cause the house of cards to collapse, if we don't do something. So, if the house of cards analogy is apt, it speaks in favor of enhancement, not against it.

The house of cards analogy isn't apt, however. It doesn't square with what we know about evolution. Organisms that were "delicately balanced" in the way a house of cards is would not be likely to survive very long, nor would a lineage comprised of such organisms be likely to persist. In the next chapter, when we examine the Extreme Connectedness Assumption—the belief that we can't throw out the bath water without losing the baby—we'll see that humans, like other organisms, have a number of features that make them quite unlike a house of cards.

Analogies can take us only so far. I wouldn't want to rest my evaluation of the challenges of biomedical enhancement on the grim tinkerer analogy. I've introduced it to expose the deep flaws of the master engineer analogy, because I think the latter distorts our reactions to the prospect of biomedical enhancement. The main point is that to come to grips with the challenges of biomedical enhancement, we need to consider it from the standpoint of evolutionary biology. Remaining stuck in the rosy old, pre-Darwinian view of nature stacks the deck against biomedical enhancement. As we'll see in later chapters, there are a number of reasons to worry about biomedical enhancement, but the risk of damaging the work of the master engineer of evolution isn't one of them.

The next chapter throws more cold water on the warm, fuzzy assumption that natural is better. As a preview of the direction it will take, consider a point Dr. Sharon Moalem makes in the wonderfully informative book *Survival of the Sickest*. She reports that around 15% of cancer-related deaths are due to *natural* toxins in our diet—that's somewhat higher than estimates of cancer-related deaths due to pesticides. Take the case of celery. Celery produces potent toxins to prevent animals and insects from eating it. Organically produced celery has *more* natural toxins than celery treated with pesticides. Why? Celery is in an arms race with predators: It has to produce ever more potent toxins to survive, because natural selection is producing predators that have resistance to its toxins. Pesticide-treated celery can survive with lower levels of natural toxins. In other words, pesticides lessen the pressures of natural selection that cause celery to produce natural toxins. So, organically produced celery may actually be more dangerous than celery treated with pesticides. The moral of this story is that natural isn't always better. In some cases, natural is better; in some cases it isn't. We need to resist the temptation to swallow overly broad generalizations and instead look at risk in a case by case fashion, utilizing our growing knowledge of how "nature" works. Presuming that natural is better is too risky. The more we learn about what in nature works for us and what doesn't, the riskier the presumption becomes.

3 | CHANGING HUMAN NATURE?

(OR: UNNATURAL ACTS,
AND NOT JUST WITH SHEEP
LIKE DOLLY)

"It is so far from being natural for a man and a woman to live in a state of marriage, that we find that all the motives which they have for remaining in that connection, and the restraints which civilized society imposes to prevent separation, are hardly sufficient to keep them together." That's James Boswell's take on the relationship between human nature and marriage in his *Life of Samuel Johnson* (1791). He doesn't say marriage is a bad idea. He only says that marriage and human nature are in opposition—that marriage is unnatural, that it goes against the grain of our natural inclinations. That's perfectly consistent with acknowledging that marriage is a good thing.

Boswell's statement reinforces something we already know from chapter 1: The fact that something is natural doesn't make it good. To say that something's natural is simply to say that it accords with the way we happen to be as a result of evolution. That includes our "natural" inclinations. Some of our natural inclinations may be bad, if they undermine what's valuable, like marriage. Nor does the fact that something is part of *human* nature make it good. After all, human nature is just the human part of nature, and as we saw in chapter 2, nature is far from being all good. Evolutionary biology explains why nature, including human nature, isn't all good.

Even before we know anything about evolution, most of us admit that human nature isn't all good and that our natural tendencies aren't always for the best. We forget all that when we think about enhancement and fall into the trap of thinking that it can't be right because it's "interfering with nature." In fact, I think it's fair to say that we tend to leave common sense behind and react reflexively, rather than reflectively, to the prospect of biomedical enhancement. There's something about a technology whose uses could be so *intimate* that dials our emotions up and our reasoning power down.

If human nature and our natural tendencies are products of evolution, it would be a miracle if they were all good. Remember, evolution isn't about what's good; if it's about anything, it's about reproductive fitness. Yet some people insist that biomedical enhancement is wrong because it might alter or destroy human nature or result in our most intimate relationships becoming "unnatural." What exactly are they talking about? Given that everything that exists is natural—part of the natural world—how could enhancements be unnatural or result in unnatural relationships?

Before we go any further, we need to note that there's a difference between altering our human nature and destroying our humanity. By our humanity, we sometimes mean what's *distinctively valuable* about us human beings. We don't want to destroy that. But not everything that is part of our human nature is valuable, much less distinctively valuable. Common sense and the major religious traditions think of human nature as a mixed bag, as we saw in chapter 2. Whether you're a pessimist or an optimist about our species depends on what you think the proportions of the mixture are, but virtually nobody thinks we are all good by nature. And most would agree that the bad parts are not minor, but rather serious.

In chapter 2 we saw that conservative guru Fukuyama worries that genetic enhancement will unwittingly destroy human nature.

I suggested that this must mean that he's really worried, not about changing human nature per se, but about tossing out the baby with the bathwater. He's merely assuming (not arguing) that the good and bad in human nature are extremely interconnected. The next chapter probes the Extreme Connectedness Assumption, by asking a simple question: Does what we know about evolution support it? The answer turns out to be "no."

Competing Concepts of Human Nature

Before we can tackle the problem of whether the good and bad parts of human nature are so extremely connected that it would be foolish to try to improve it, we need to be clear about what we mean by human nature. We also need to determine what, if anything, human nature can tell us about what we ought or ought not to do. That's what this chapter does.

There are two very good reasons why we ought to take the time to figure out what we mean by human nature when we're thinking about enhancement, or anything else, for that matter. The first is that lots of intelligent people throughout history have been deeply mistaken about what is and isn't human nature. They've confused nature with nurture and made the mistake of thinking that how people are nurtured—or as we say now, acculturated—in *their* society is the way people are everywhere.

The concept of human nature is still controversial today. In fact, it's more controversial than ever, because science is increasingly challenging our commonsense ideas about what is and what isn't human nature. There's no excuse for any reasonably educated person in the twenty-first century to rely naïvely on this problematic concept. Yet as we'll see, prominent participants in the debate about biomedical enhancement do just that with depressing regularity.

The second reason we need to clarify what we mean by human nature is that there's a long, shameful record of people using talk about human nature and the natural to demean and oppress people who are different. For example, homosexuals have been branded as committing crimes against nature, engaging in unnatural acts. We have to be wary of people imposing their subjective values on others under the cloak of seemingly objective statements about what's natural and what isn't.

This is precisely what's going on when some Christian fundamentalists say that by its very nature marriage is a union between a man and a woman. It may be true that the word "marriage" has been defined that way in dictionaries and functions that way in common usage. That's hardly surprising, because until recently marriage as a social practice has been limited to males being married to females. But that doesn't mean that same-sex marriage is unnatural in any sense, much less that it's bad because it is unnatural. Recall Boswell's statement: Marriage, by which he meant marriage between a man and a woman, is unnatural. Boswell was probably too uncritical about his ability to distinguish between nature and nurture, but at least he didn't make the mistake of thinking that branding something as unnatural shows it's bad.

Criticizing something by saying it's unnatural or contrary to human nature is cheating. More precisely, it's what's known in the retail trade as bait and switch: You start out supposedly talking about how things *are* (what our nature is, what's natural) and then slip in your own values about the way things *should* be. It's a kind of stealth moral imperialism. Given the danger that talk about human nature and the natural can be co-opted in this way, it's useful to begin with a quick survey of different understandings of human nature.

For Aristotle, human nature is something permanent and universal in all humans: a set of characteristics we all have and that distinguishes us from other animals. For him, the idea of changing our nature makes no sense. If we lost some of these *essential* characteristics, we wouldn't be humans; in fact, *we* would no longer exist. That's what it means to say they are essential.

Given that evolution is ceaseless change, there's not much to be said for a conception of human nature that assumes permanence. From the standpoint of evolutionary biology, human nature is the basic biological makeup of members of the species *Homo sapiens* at this point in its evolution. Traditionally, species are distinguished by frontiers of interfertility: Members of the same species can produce offspring together; members of different species can't. Notice that "can't" here is short for "can't by unassisted reproduction." We saw in chapter 2 that this isn't an obstacle to new genetic combinations, now that we have genetic engineering and reproductive technologies like IVF.

Suppose we equate natures (human nature, chimp nature, and so on) with the distinctive characteristics of various species. The crucial point is that from an evolutionary perspective, species come and go. So human nature, whatever that is, will be replaced by some kind of post-human nature if we don't go extinct before passing on the torch. That's important to remember when you hear someone like Fukuyama saying that we are in danger of destroying human nature if we engage in intentional genetic modification. Human nature will eventually be destroyed if we *don't* use intentional genetic modification; unintentional genetic modification will see to that. Ironically, IGM might be the only way to preserve human nature.

Notice also that there's no guarantee that UGM will preserve the parts of human nature we value most. What it's likely to preserve are the parts of human nature that are conducive to

reproductive fitness and that may or may not include what we value most about ourselves.

Anthropologists and social psychologists sometimes operate with a different notion of human nature, one that includes cultural as well as biological characteristics. Those who hold this view of human nature think there are some culturally produced traits that are universal among all humans or at least very widely shared (at this point in history). Like those who hold a strictly biological conception, they make room for the possibility that human nature can change, either in its biological component or its cultural component, or both.

Is Human Nature (Now) Partly Cultural?

The idea that there could be a cultural component of human nature will be puzzling to you if you operate on the assumption that the distinction between what's part of our nature and what isn't corresponds exactly to the old nature/nurture distinction. According to one way of understanding that distinction, nature is pure biology. Everything else, including culture, is nurture. But that's not the only way. Instead, we can think of human nature as a set of characteristics that have four properties: (1) they help to distinguish us from other animals; (2) they are very widespread among mature, undamaged *homo sapiens*; (3) they play an important role in explaining human behavior; and (4) they are deeply entrenched in the sense that it's very hard—if not impossible—*once the individual has developed them*, to eradicate them by education or indoctrination. This last feature is important, when you think of how we talk about human nature. For example, we say things like "It's just human nature that people are self-interested and any economic system that doesn't recognize that can't work." The implication is that efforts to create the new

"communist man" won't work, no matter how vigorous the indoctrination program is. A culturally produced characteristic could satisfy all four criteria if it was inculcated early enough in the individual's development and was strongly supported by peer pressure and social practices. So traits that are the product of nurture, if they satisfy (1)–(4), could be considered part of human nature. Given how important culture has become for defining who we are and how we differ from other animals, this makes good sense.

Using a notion of human nature that makes room for cultural traits is useful for evaluating worries about biomedical enhancements changing or destroying human nature. Sometimes, those who have these worries are concerned about biological changes per se, but sometimes they worry about biological changes destroying cultural traits that they think are very valuable. For example, as we'll see later, Bush's Council on Bioethics and its chairman, the physician-bioethicist Leon Kass, think of human nature as including certain very specific relationships between men and women and between children and parents. They worry that if biomedical enhancements become widespread, these valuable relationships will be damaged. We needn't read them as saying that these relationships are purely biological; they may be culturally evolved relationships, though they're based in biology. Bush's Council apparently thinks these relationships are so vital to a good human life that they are in effect part of our nature or what's natural for us. They worry that biomedical enhancements, especially genetic enhancements, will destroy these relationships and replace them with relationships that are unnatural, not really *human*.

The Moral Imperialist Bait and Switch

There's something fishy about the way the Council proceeds. Why do they think the way to stress that something's highly valuable is

to say that it's part of human nature or natural human relations? That would only make sense if human nature or natural human relations are always good. If human nature and natural human relations are simply what we are like because of our evolutionary history, then there's no reason to believe they're good. In fact, what we learned about evolution in chapter 2 should make us think that at least some of nature, including the part of nature we call human nature, isn't good.

Why should we think it's any different with cultural traits? Anthropologists provide plenty of evidence that some deeply entrenched social practices are not only morally disgusting, but downright destructive. Here's one example among many. Among the Ilahita Arapesh, a tribe in New Guinea, there's a deeply entrenched social practice requiring men to gorge themselves even when this means that their wives and children are chronically hungry and malnourished. This behavior is very stressful for the men, who sometimes become physically sick as a result. But the social taboo on sharing food equitably with your wife and children is so strong that men continue to act in a way that literally makes them ill and condemns their families to misery. Whether this practice was ever valuable seems dubious, but it certainly isn't now. It's an abomination.

Female genital mutilation (female genital cutting, for the politically correct) may be easier to explain as an adaptation. Perhaps the first women to undergo this ghastly procedure achieved a gain in reproductive fitness through the mechanism of sexual selection. In evolutionary terms, the excision of the clitoris served as a signal to the male that this woman was not likely to spread other guys' genes (mainly because she wouldn't enjoy sex enough to fool around). But once the practice became universal, it obviously couldn't play this role in sexual selection: If all women have it, it can't signal that any particular woman is special. Yet a woman who refrains from the practice would be at a reproductive disadvantage, because no one would want to marry her. That would explain why a practice that seems to benefit no one and causes so much misery could persist. There may be other, complementary explanations, too. For example, the fact that societies are male-dominated presumably helps explain why the practice persists.

The moral of these grisly stories is that although cultural practices, like biological traits, can get selected for and become entrenched, that doesn't mean they're good. It doesn't even mean that they are conducive to the survival of the society. As Jared Diamond has shown, sometimes cultural practices can cause the death of a society, by destroying the environment the society depends on. Remember, to say something is an adaptation just says something about how it came about, nothing about its present value. That holds for cultural adaptations as well as biological ones.

The Bush Council isn't earning its anti-enhancement conclusions honestly. They're engaging in bait and switch, smuggling in their own value judgments under the cover of seemingly objective assertions about human nature and the natural. If they want to show that we shouldn't enhance because doing so will damage valuable relationships, they need to first establish that the relationships are valuable. In fact, they have to show more than that: They have to show that they are *uniquely* valuable, that there's only one valuable way to be married, only one valuable form of child-parent relationship, etc. And then they need to show that enhancement puts these uniquely valuable particular forms of relationships seriously at risk. They never do any of this, however. They simply assert that if we use genetic enhancements, this will undermine the natural relationship between men and women, and create a new, inhuman world brimming with unnatural relationships.

Take the example of human cloning—producing a human being by Dolly the sheep–style nuclear transfer cloning. Here's how it works. First you take an egg cell and remove its nucleus (the dense core that contains the whole complement of DNA for the animal whose egg cell it is). Then you take a nucleus from a body cell of another animal—in Dolly's case a cell from the mammary gland (that's why she was named after Dolly Parton). Next you bring the egg cell without its own nucleus together with the nucleus from the body cell and zap them with an electric current. The current breaks down the egg cell's outer wall, fuses the body cell nucleus into the egg cell, and triggers the process of cell division. If all goes well, you get a new animal that has a unique characteristic: Unlike the rest of us, it gets all its DNA, not just half, from one individual. Cloning is asexual reproduction. Sexual reproduction involves creating an individual using the DNA from a male and a female parent; cloning uses just one parent, genetically speaking.

The Bush Council says that human cloning isn't *human* procreation, because it isn't sexual reproduction and human reproduction is sexual. On the face of it, that's an odd thing to say. If it's a human being that's produced, what else could it be but human procreation? What's happened here is that they're covertly shifting between two different senses of the term "human"—using it in a purely descriptive sense in the phrase "human cloning" (to mean cloning of a human being) and in a covertly evaluative or judgmental sense in the phrase "human procreation" (to mean the only correct way for humans to reproduce). In asserting that producing a human by cloning isn't human procreation, they're making a negative value judgment about asexual reproduction but disguising it as a factual claim. It's a controversial value judgment and they're just asserting it, not arguing in support of it. This is not just moral imperialism; it's stealth moral imperialism.

Notice what kind of value judgment it is. They aren't just implying that asexual reproduction is *less good* than sexual reproduction or even that asexual reproduction is *wrong*. They are suggesting something far stronger: that it's *wrong in an especially serious way*—namely, that it's less than human, that it violates our human dignity. They're implying that asexual reproduction *debases* us, in something like the way we think having sex with animals debases us. The implications for a person who is produced by asexual reproduction aren't very pleasant: They are tainted by their origins, perhaps not fully human.

Kass and company also indulge in another style of argument that is just as dubious. They insinuate that the only reasons most people would have for producing a human by cloning are unseemly—for example, to act out a sick fantasy of recreating their dead child from the DNA in a strand of hair or to indulge their narcissism. There are other, quite respectable reasons someone might want to reproduce this way. For example, a female graduate student told me that she would definitely consider cloning—if it were perfectly safe (or at least as safe as ordinary human reproduction)—if she was at the stage of her life when she wanted a child but didn't have a partner. Under these conditions, she said, "I would prefer cloning to IVF." There were several things about IVF that bothered her: its high failure rate, its physical invasiveness, the possible increased risk of cancer from the hormone cocktail you take to stimulate ovulation, and the problem of what to do with surplus embryos. But she was also concerned about sperm donation. She said she would rather produce a child with DNA from just one parent than "borrow" a sperm from somebody that wasn't her partner.

She wasn't worried about having a child that was "just like her" because she knew enough about genetics to avoid the Xerox copy fallacy—thinking that an individual who is genetically identical to you is identical to you. That's a fallacy because a person isn't her genes; she's a complex, unpredictable result of the interaction of her genes and her environment and, at a certain point, she becomes in part a product of her own choices. You might disagree with this young woman about cloning, but there's no call to accuse her of contemplating an unnatural act.

Not content to say that asexual reproduction is less than human, Kass and company go on to suggest that even in the case of old-fashioned sexual reproduction, unless a baby is the product of "love" rather than of "an act of will," this isn't human procreation. This extraordinary assertion has the implication that if a man and a woman have a child in order to have an heir or, as in very poor countries with no welfare systems, to have someone to support them in old age, they aren't engaging in *human* procreation—they are acting in a subhuman, debasing way. It's the same old bait and switch: Kass et al. are sliding from their value judgment that it is *best* for children to be conceived in love (a plausible claim) to the seemingly descriptive but actually evaluative statement that unless that's how children are conceived we are in the terrain of the less than human, the realm of debasement, rubbing shoulders with those who have sex with sheep or corpses (or sheep corpses).

I've heard this sort of demeaning, moral imperialist talk before. I heard it a great deal when I was a child growing up in Arkansas in the 1950s. That society was deeply racist and the racism was institutionalized: Southern-style apartheid or, as it's more commonly known, Jim Crow. White people down there thought that marriage between whites and blacks was unnatural in the sense of being debasing (for whites), because they thought blacks were naturally inferior, that they belonged to a lower order. Similarly, some people today think that same-sex marriage is unnatural and what they really mean is that it's inferior, not fully human. The implications for gays and lesbians are equally demeaning.

Simple honesty demands avoiding the moral imperialist bait and switch. If Kass and company think that certain ways of procreating or of marrying are uniquely valuable, there's no need to say they are natural. Just say they are uniquely valuable and then do something serious to support that claim. That's just the beginning of the task they face, however. They've then got to show why people ought to be required, as a matter of law, to engage in the very best form of marriage or not be married at all. Showing that heterosexual marriage is the ideal form of marriage is a long way from showing that same-sex marriage shouldn't be legally recognized.

The lesson for thinking about biomedical enhancement is clear. Suppose you're worried about genetically engineering human embryos to improve human capacities. Don't say that this is not human reproduction or that it's unnatural. Explain what's wrong with it. That's harder, but at least it's honest work. The remaining chapters of this book take up this task. The next chapter grapples with what I believe to be the most serious concern about biomedical enhancements: the risk of unintended bad biological consequences.

Human Nature as a Constraint on Morality

Kass and company aren't the first to try to determine what's right and wrong by appealing to human nature. The history of moral philosophy is littered with the wreckage of failed attempts to do that. I think it's fair to say that there's a general consensus nowadays among people who think systematically about ethics that we shouldn't expect the idea of human nature to yield answers to substantive moral issues like whether we should use biomedical enhancements or whether there are cases in which it would be morally permissible to reproduce by cloning. Careful thinkers tend to agree that the role for appeals to nature and the natural in ethics is more limited. Many think that human nature makes morality—or at least a full-blown kind of morality—possible. They also think that human nature shapes the general contours of morality. But they don't think human nature gives us detailed moral marching orders.

One way human nature might shape the general contours of morality is by setting limits to what it's reasonable for us to demand of ourselves, morally speaking. In simplest terms, this is the old slogan "Ought implies Can." (Not to be confused with what my old teacher, the late and lamented Sidney Morgenbesser, called the first principle of Jewish ethics: "Can implies Shouldn't!")

"Ought implies Can" means that you aren't obligated to do what isn't possible for you to do. It turns out that this slogan has some interesting exceptions, but when applied to the connection between human nature and morality, it's intuitively plausible. For example, suppose it's true, as some psychologists say, that there's a significant emotional component to human beings' decisions about what to do when they face certain moral problems. For example, our feelings of outrage when we see a blatant case of racial discrimination may prompt us to act, rather than just passively stand by and watch it happen.

Because of our evolved nature, we can't make such decisions without relying on our emotional responses; that's just the way human moral decision-making is. A morality that required us to decide in a purely calculating, cognitive manner, with no role for emotions, wouldn't be realistic. To be appropriate for human beings, a morality must take human nature into account. More specifically, it has to take human psychology into account, as my colleague, the highly original philosopher Owen Flanagan, famously argued a decade and a half ago.

Some of the most interesting work in philosophical ethics attempts to work out the implications of this insight. Some of that work prematurely concludes that commonsense morality or traditional moral theories expect too much of us. This conclusion is premature because those who draw it take too literally the idea that the evolved constraints on morality are "hardwired." That suggests that there's no way of getting around them. A simple example will show why an evolved psychological tendency needn't be like that.

Psychologists have found that errors in probabilistic reasoning are pervasive. A notorious example is the gambler's fallacy: thinking that if you've lost several times in a row, you're due for a win. Suppose that there's a good evolutionary explanation for why human beings tend to make this mistake. It would be wrong to conclude that if this is an evolved cognitive error it is "hardwired" in the sense that we can't work around it. We can work around it, by being on the alert that we are prone to make it and then calculating the odds using simple probability theory rather than following our erroneous gut instincts.

Here's another example: traditional methods of memory training, writing, and, more recently, electronic recording technologies such as audio and videotapes and computer disks. These are all used to help counteract evolved flaws in human memory. Or think of moral principles or simple rules of prudence or rational self-interest. These can be seen as techniques we've developed to counter our "natural" tendencies to follow our destructive impulses, or to fail to think about the distant consequences of what we do, or about what it would be like to be on the receiving end of our actions.

Consider two examples, one prudential—having to do with what's in our own best interest—the other having to do with the morality of our treatment of others. In his fascinating book *How We Decide*, Jonah Lehrer notes that psychologists believe that we have an evolved tendency to go for immediate rewards while failing to appreciate the future costs. In a world where it's all too easy to get a credit card, this trait can be disastrous. The self-help sections of bookstores are filled with techniques for how to counteract this tendency, and some of them work. These techniques can be seen as enhancements of our unfortunately limited evolved capacity for making wise decisions. Or consider the Golden Rule: It's a technique for enhancing our capacity to make good moral decisions. Using it forces us to consider the well-being of others, not just our own. The same is true for Kant's Categorical Imperative and Adam Smith's thought experiment of taking the perspective of an impartial spectator who considers the effects of a proposed action on all who will be affected.

Recall that I said that some philosophers draw premature conclusions from the fact that our evolved nature includes certain emotional and cognitive limitations. They conclude that most moral theories, and perhaps commonsense morality as well, are too demanding because they ignore these limitations. That *might* be true, but showing that it's true becomes more complicated, once we see that we can use various enhancement techniques to work around those limitations.

So far, the enhancement techniques haven't been biomedical. In the future, they may well be. For example, the philosopher-physician Thomas Douglas argues that we should take seriously the possibility of biomedical moral enhancement. It may be possible to develop drugs that increase our ability to empathize with others, for example. There is already evidence that people become more trusting and cooperative if you increase the level of the hormone oxytocin in their brains.

Alternatively, if it turns out that some of our moral errors are the result of our having beliefs that arise through faulty reasoning processes, cognitive enhancements might have the welcome side effect of making us more likely to do the right thing. The point is that the more we learn about how our evolved limitations work, the more amenable they will become to biomedical interventions. Biomedical enhancements could be especially powerful tools for overcoming the evolved traits that make it hard to live up to our moral principles (or our commitment to prudence). Hardwiring that can be rewired isn't hard in any interesting sense.

Let's rephrase Boswell's remark about marriage in the language of evolved constraints. Perhaps humans have evolved to have some traits that make marriage hard going. For example, suppose it's true that males are "hardwired" to spread their genes around and this increases the risk of infidelity. ("Honey, don't blame me; it was my selfish genes . . .") In chapter 6, I'll examine the fascinating prospect of biomedically enhancing our capacity for fidelity: the case of "love drugs," or more accurately drugs that would enhance human "pair-bonding."

If a "hardwired" tendency toward infidelity in males does exist, it doesn't follow that we should adjust our morality accordingly and cut guys some slack. Perhaps the moral thing to do is to try to counteract this tendency. The first step would be to dispense with the "hardwiring" talk, which smacks of crude genetic determinism, and recognize that what we are dealing with is a tendency, not an inevitability. As the examples above indicate, we have a lot of tendencies that we can counteract or work around. There's no need to assume that the best way to work around an evolved constraint will always utilize biomedical interventions, but there's also no need to assume that it never will.

Contemporary philosophers who think that the implications of evolved constraints on human cognitive and emotional performance for ethics are straightforward are therefore mistaken. Even if ethical theory (or commonsense morality) doesn't explicitly recognize these limitations, it doesn't follow that it is unrealistic. That will depend on whether we can utilize enhancements, whether biomedical nor nonbiomedical, to narrow the gap between what a morality demands and what we can do. Some moral theories—for example, those that utilize decision techniques like the Golden Rule or Kant's Categorical Imperative—already do this. In the future, biomedical technologies may provide much more powerful tools. Perhaps our distant descendants will say that our morality was embarrassingly undemanding. If we fail to utilize biomedical enhancements to work around evolved constraints, they may say that we were morally at fault for acquiescing to our limitations.

I noted earlier that the history of ethics is replete with failed attempts to draw substantive moral guidance from a concept of human nature. Contemporary philosophers of the sort I've described are trying to do something similar, but in a negative way. They argue that by reflecting on the emotional and cognitive limitations of our evolved nature we can draw conclusions about what morality *can't* require of us. But if—because of our evolved limitations—morality can't require us to refrain from doing X, then something substantive does follow, namely, that *it is morally permissible to do X*. That looks like success in doing something that philosophers have failed to do in the past, namely, drawing substantive moral conclusions from an understanding of human nature. I've just argued, however, that getting from a description of our evolved limitations to conclusions about what morality can reasonably require of us isn't that simple. But even if the missing steps could be supplied, it seems unlikely that any such general view about the relationship between our "natural" limitations and the possible content of morality could be fine-grained enough to answer questions about whether we should undertake this or that biomedical enhancement.

Conservative bioethicists appeal in vain to vague, covertly evaluative notions of human nature, uninformed by an understanding of evolution, to try to condemn biomedical enhancement. Human nature *is* relevant to the enhancement debate, but not in the way they think. We can't derive anti-enhancement conclusions from a scientific understanding of human nature. But if we acknowledge that our nature is a product of evolution and recognize the constraints under which it operates, we may be led to the conclusion that we *should* employ biomedical enhancements. Suppose that some aspects of our current evolved nature make it harder for us to live well or to live up to our moral principles. Surely we should try to overcome these limitations through the use of biomedical science or whatever else works, not simply accept them and trim back our morality to ensure a good fit.

Some philosophers who explore the implications of our evolved traits on moral theory use the language of human nature, but many don't. They are rightly suspicious of such talk, given its dismal track record. They also may believe that they don't need to talk about human nature. That's correct: We can make the point that there are evolved limitations (at present) on our emotional and cognitive responses without taking a stand on the disputed topic of human nature. All that really matters is whether limitations exist—and whether we can alter them—not whether they are part of our essence or definitive of our species.

Human Good and Human Nature

There's one more concern about human nature worth considering. Even if we can't derive substantive moral decisions by reflecting on human nature, perhaps there is a vital link between human nature and value—or what philosophers call "the good." Aristotle thought there was. He thought that an important part of our human nature is rationality. He concluded that whatever else a good human life is like, it has to allow considerable scope for the exercise of rationality. Similarly, he thought that because humans are social by nature, a good human life must include ample opportunities for social interactions.

Thinking along these lines, we arrive at the conclusion that there is a crucial link between human nature and human good. Surely what's good for a human being isn't what's good for a dog or a cat. Some contemporary philosophers, including Martha Nussbaum, who acknowledges a debt to Aristotle, argue that human nature includes the potential for engaging in various activities and that a good human life is one in which people can effectively engage in these activities if they choose. The main point is that making judgments about what is good for humans only makes sense against the background of assumptions about what human beings are like.

If that's correct, then a disturbing prospect immediately comes into view. If we change (or destroy) human nature, won't we lose the ability to know what's good? The worry is that if we become something other than human, we won't have a benchmark or yardstick by which to determine what's valuable. Or, to use another metaphor: We'll lose our evaluative anchor and be adrift, unable to judge what is good and what is bad.

If the change from human to post-human nature through biomedical enhancements were gradual enough, this might not be a problem. If we don't succumb to some man-made or "natural" disaster and go extinct very rapidly, then ordinary, unassisted evolution will lead to post-human nature replacing human nature. Aristotle's point will hold for post-humans: What's good for them will depend on post-human nature. The fact that there aren't any beings whose nature is human won't interfere with *their* ability to judge the good. So a gradual process, the only sort that evolution is usually capable of, would avoid a situation in which beings who care about the good don't have a clue as to what it is, because their bench-mark for judging good has instantly disappeared. Notice again that we don't have to frame this point in the language of human nature. All that really matters is whether there are some very widespread and deeply entrenched features of human beings at present that pro-vide a kind of reference point for our judgments about value. Nonetheless, I'll continue to use that language, because I'm consid-ering objections to enhancement and the critics of enhancement tend to rely on it.

What about a change from human to post-human nature that occurred much more rapidly, as a result of widespread biomedical enhancements? That might be more problematic, but only if there weren't significant continuities between human nature and post-human nature. It's hard to imagine that there wouldn't be significant continuities between the way we are now and the way we would try to become through biomedical enhancements. If we lived longer, were smarter, healthier, more capable of empathizing with others, we wouldn't be extraterrestrial aliens—we'd be enhanced humans. If the result of enhancement is ramped up versions of capacities we now value, why *wouldn't* we know how to value them?

This isn't to say that there would be no change in our under-standing of what counts as a good life. Presumably, in a world where biomedical enhancements were common, we'd have higher stan-dards. But that's true of our current world, as compared with that of our not-so-distant ancestors. When half of children died young and most people hovered just above subsistence, suffering from chronic parasitic diseases and with a much higher probability of dying a violent death, the standards for a good life were presumably lower. Yet progress hasn't caused us to lose our grip on what "good" means.

There's a deeper point here. It may be true that our present under-standing of what's valuable is linked to our present nature—it's hard to see how it could be otherwise. But the link may not be so tight as we assume when we worry that changing our nature will undercut our ability to judge goodness. Remember, we're drawn toward enhancement because we recognize that human nature has some serious flaws. We're making a judgment that our human nature is not all good. That means that we already have a conception of goodness that is to some extent *independent* of our nature. More paradoxically, one feature of our nature is that we are able to make judgments about its goodness. But if that is so, then there's a sense in which our ability to make judgments about value isn't tied so closely to how we are now. We already have a sense of value that enables us to occupy a standpoint that is partly beyond our present nature. If we change the right parts of our nature, this shouldn't negatively impact our ability to judge what's good. Even changing ourselves *radically*, so that we were post-human, wouldn't deprive us of the ability to judge the good; it would equip us with a basis for making judgments about the good *for post-humans*.

Summing Up

In this chapter, I've explored attempts to appeal to human nature and the natural in the debate about biomedical enhancement. I've argued that the concept of human nature has always been controversial, but has become increasingly so as our scientific knowledge increases. Some of the worries people try to express when they say we shouldn't alter human nature or that biomedical enhancements would undermine natural relationships may be valid. But there's nothing to be gained and a lot to be lost by presenting them in these terms. *Anything of value for the enhancement debate can be said without invoking nature and the natural.* Given how controversial statements about what is and isn't part of human nature are, trying to resolve thorny controversies about enhancement by invoking human nature is like trying to shore up a teetering skyscraper with a glob of Jell-O. Even worse, there's a long, depressing history of appeals to human nature being used to disguise erroneous factual claims and portray some peoples' preferences as if they were objective values. Finally, rhetoric about what's unnatural or contrary to human nature is typically used to demean and devalue those who are different. For all of these reasons, it's better to avoid appeals to human nature and the natural in the enhancement debate and rely instead on the best available scientific knowledge we have about what human beings are like now.

One valid concern that is sometimes framed (unnecessarily) in terms of human nature is the worry about Extreme Connectedness—the risk of throwing out the baby with the bathwater. We *should* be concerned about the possibility that in attempting to improve ourselves we will unwittingly do damage. The problem of unintended bad consequences is a serious one— in my judgment, the most serious one we face as we stand on the threshold of the era of biomedical enhancements. Dispensing with confusing rhetoric about human nature, we can formulate the issue this way: On the basis of what we know about our biology, can we ameliorate some of our bad features without creating an unacceptable risk of destroying our good ones? That question is one important aspect of the next chapter's topic. It examines the problem of unintended bad consequences of enhancement.

4 | PLAYING GOD, RESPONSIBLY

If we want things to stay as they are, things will have to change.

Change for Stability, Enhancement for Preservation

The paradoxical quote above is the most famous line in a justly famous novel, *The Leopard*, by Giuseppe di Lampedusa. This work, written in the 1950s but set in 1860, explores the meaning of conservatism. The main character, Don Fabrizio (played by Burt Lancaster in the movie version), is a Sicilian nobleman who wants to preserve his traditional aristocratic life and the social preeminence of his family. But he lives in revolutionary times, during the Risorgimento, the violent, chaotic struggle to unify Italy. His nephew, Tancredi, makes a simple point about the complexity of being a conservative: Conservatism is about cherishing and sustaining the good things passed on to us from previous generations, but sometimes we have to make changes to do that. Don Fabrizio's predicament is that he's unsure which changes will preserve the world he cherishes—and which will destroy it.

Our situation is even more complicated. Like Don Fabrizio, we want to preserve what's good; but we also realize that we have remarkable new opportunities for improving human life by biomedical means. Simpleminded conservatives think we can choose not to change—that we can just say no. Tancredi knows otherwise: He understands not only that change is inevitable, but also that sometimes we have to change in order to preserve. Naïve (or uncharitable) conservatives like Michael Sandel assume that the pursuit of enhancement signals a greedy dissatisfaction with the status quo, an insatiable appetite for perfection. Tancredi sees that this is wrong, too. He knows that we sometimes seek to improve aspects of our world, not because we're dissatisfied with the status quo, but because we want to protect it.

Remember, enhancement is capacity-relative: To enhance is to improve some particular capacity. We may need to improve some particular capacity in order to preserve what we value. So there's nothing inconsistent about the idea that enhancement can aim at sustaining the status quo rather than improving on it. The debate about biomedical enhancement looks very different if we keep Tancredi's insight in mind.

In chapter 1 we encountered one case where biomedical enhancements may be needed just to help ensure that we don't experience a *decline* in average quality of life. The cumulative effect of the historical enhancements I described in chapter 1, when taken together with medical advances, has created a situation in which more and more people are living much longer. But because natural selection doesn't winnow out undesirable post-reproductive traits, this means decades more of declining mental and physical health. Whether your life goes well depends on its quality across the whole span of your life. If we routinely live to 110 but spend the last twenty years in a downward spiral of pain and disability, we'll be worse off than we are now. The personal and economic consequences of this scenario are almost too dreadful to contemplate.

Something will have to be done. An effective response will be multipronged, but it is overwhelmingly likely that one component of it will involve biomedical enhancements. Boosting the normal capacity of tissue to regenerate and ramping up tumor-suppressing genes to resist the tendency for aging cells to turn cancerous are only two possibilities among many. We'll need biomedical enhancements to cope with the negative unintended consequences of medical advances we've already made.

Here are several additional examples of biomedical enhancements that could help us sustain the good we now enjoy or, to put it negatively, prevent things from getting worse.

1. Enhancement of existing capacities for impulse control, sympathy, altruism, or moral imagination, through pharmaceutical or other biomedical interventions. Our propensity for violence and xenophobia, combined with the availability of weapons of mass destruction, makes us highly vulnerable. Biomedical enhancements may be one component of a strategy for avoiding catastrophic violence. This doesn't assume that violence is "biologically determined" in some rigid, mechanistic fashion. It only assumes that biomedical interventions can have a positive impact, if combined with other interventions. There's no "altruism gene" anymore than there's a "fat gene" or a "gay gene"—that's a gross simplification of the complex relationships involved. But there may be genetic modifications, or much more likely, drugs that can help strengthen our capacity for altruism or at least for trust. In fact, as I've already noted, there's evidence that increasing the levels of oxytocin in our brains promotes trust.

2. Enhancement of the capacity to extract nutrients from existing foods. More radically, enhancing our digestive and metabolic capacities to enable us to eat items that humans have never been able to consume before. (Notice that we've already done this in a low-tech way: Cooking makes food more digestible and enables extraction of more calories per volume of food. It also neutralizes

toxins and thereby enables us to safely eat what would otherwise be deadly. Once again, biomedical enhancements can be viewed as on a continuum with other enhancements we've already achieved.)

3. Enhancement of the viability of human gametes (sperm and eggs) or embryos, or the invention of enhanced reproductive technologies, to counteract a drastic decrease in fertility or in lethal mutations caused by accumulating toxins in the environment. (Think here of the film *Children of Men*, which depicts a world where infertility has become the norm, presumably due to pollution.)

4. Enhancements of the immune system to help us better resist emerging pandemics in an era of globalization.

5. Enhancements to improve the body's capacity for thermal regulation, in the face of severe climate change.

6. Enhancement of the capacity of skin cells to resist cancer, if the ozone layer becomes dangerously depleted.

I don't know whether we'll develop any of these particular interventions. They're only intended to illustrate that Tancredi's insight applies to biomedical enhancements.

Some people might object that it's wrong to use "technological fixes" for the problems we create—that instead we should correct the deeper social problems that cause them. That may be true in some cases. For example, instead of dying everybody's skin white to avoid racial stereotyping, we should keep striving to overcome prejudice. But sometimes employing technology to solve problems is not only permissible, but obligatory. That's true when the only solution that can be achieved quickly enough requires technology. That could be the case with emerging pandemics or toxins that cause infertility or the depletion of the ozone layer.

Extreme Connectedness

Biomedical enhancements are here and more are on the way, so we have to think hard about the risk of unintended bad consequences. But first we have to think about *how* to think about this risk. Avoiding the naïve conservative's fallacy of thinking that enhancement is just about improvement or perfection, rather than about holding our own is a step in the right direction. What else do we need to do?

Several things. First we need to examine an assumption that most anti-enhancement types seem to make, but that they never defend: the assumption that the various aspects of a human being are so closely tied to one another that if we use biomedical interventions to try to improve ourselves, we'll make things worse. We first encountered this assumption in chapter 2 when we saw that Fukuyama thinks eliminating the bad parts of human nature would unconscionably endanger the good parts. If you assume Extreme Connectedness, you'll quickly conclude that biomedical enhancements are too risky.

People who worry about unintended bad consequences tend to think the problem is most severe in the case of genetic enhancements. In the previous chapter, I argued that genetic enhancement (intentional genetic modification, IGM) has some striking advantages over evolution as usual (unintentional genetic modification, UGM), when it comes to improving or even sustaining human life. But if the human organism is internally very densely interconnected—if it's like a seamless web—then we may not be able to ameliorate our worst features without destroying the best. Are we really like seamless webs? Will snipping one thread cause the whole thing to unravel?

Throughout the ages, conservative thinkers have assumed that the various components of society are densely interconnected.

They've pictured society as a seamless web, warning that any effort at large-scale social reform is doomed to catastrophic failure. For example, fifty years ago there was a public debate in the UK over whether the laws that made "homosexual behavior" in public a crime should be struck down. A member of the House of Lords, Sir Patrick Devlin, argued that without these laws the moral underpinnings of society would collapse. The laws were struck down and Devlin turned out to be wrong (unless you count allowing homosexual behavior in public as itself constituting the collapse of society!). Devlin didn't present sociological evidence to show that society was such a seamless web that changing these laws would make the whole bloody thing unravel. He couldn't have, because the evidence didn't exist and still doesn't.

Bioconservatives are just like Lord Devlin. They assert that biomedical enhancements (or at least those that involve genetic changes) are likely to cause us to unravel, but they dodge the crucial issue: Is there scientific evidence that the human organism is that densely interconnected? So their central argument for not trying to improve ourselves isn't really an argument. It's only an assertion, a conclusion in search of a crucial premise.

Let's take stock of where we are. In chapter 1, I began to make the case that biomedical enhancements could be very beneficial. I also showed that enhancement isn't new and that biomedical enhancements aren't so different from past enhancements as to be in a different moral category altogether. In chapter 2, I pointed out that evolution doesn't do such a good job and that intentional genetic modification could do better. In this chapter so far, I've shown that biomedical enhancements may be needed just to keep things from getting a whole lot worse. Taken together, all this makes a pretty strong prima facie case for being receptive to the idea of biomedical enhancements. It's only a prima facie case, because we'd still have to look at proposed biomedical enhancements case by case, carefully weighing the pros and cons, in the light of the best evidence about risks as well as benefits.

If the Extreme Connectedness Assumption were true—if the human organism were like a seamless web—then the prima facie case for biomedical enhancements would collapse. Game over. So a lot depends on whether that assumption is true. We might not be in a position to know for certain whether it's true, however. But at least we should find out whether it's a *justified* assumption. There's only one way to do that: Look at what biology tells us about how we are constructed. That means looking at how evolution concocts critters like us.

Recall what we learned about evolution in chapter 2: Organisms are constantly "trying" to adapt to new challenges, because the environment is ever-changing. The master evolutionary biologist Van Valen (not the master guitarist Van Halen) used a vivid metaphor to capture this situation: An organism is like the Red Queen in *Through the Looking Glass*, who has to keep running faster and faster, as the ground crumbles beneath her, just to stay where she is. If that's our situation, then we need to be resilient, not fragile.

It's hard to see how we could have survived as long as we have, or for any appreciable length of time at all, if snipping one thread would cause us to unravel completely. Seamless web organisms wouldn't have a chance. In fact, it's highly unlikely—virtually impossible—that evolution would produce organisms like that in the first place. The point is that *natural selection can't work on seamless webs*. It works only if there can be incremental changes. It only works, that is, if an organism can change one of its traits without changing the others. It's because traits *don't* hang so closely together that organisms can replace old traits with new ones without falling apart.

So much for the poor fit between the idea of natural selection and the assumption that organisms are like fragile, seamless webs. Quite apart from that, there are three more concrete facts about evolution that make the seamless web idea look pretty dubious. Before explaining them, I can't resist a "gotcha" comment aimed at bioconservatives who say biomedical enhancement is too risky for fragile, seamless webs like us. If we're that fragile, perhaps our only hope is to enhance ourselves to be more resilient! Maybe this is yet another case where we may need enhancements just to prevent things from getting worse, a whole lot worse.

I don't have to place much weight on this "gotcha," because there are three basic features of evolved organisms that undermine the Extreme Connectedness Assumption. They show that it can't bear the weight bioconservatives put on it.

The first is that evolved organisms show a lot of *modularity*. By definition, a module is a subsystem that has denser connections among its own parts than it does with things around it. Given how evolution works, it's not surprising that we see a lot of modularity. Here's one example: As an embryo develops into a mature organism, the process creates "firewalls" that make it more likely that things will turn out well. If something goes wrong in one module, the damage can be contained within it, without the whole thing going haywire. Modules are designed to prevent unraveling. They do this by making sure that organisms aren't seamless. The boundaries of modules are seams.

Given what organisms have to face (remember the Red Queen), it's not hard to see that modularization would be selected for. Modularization is a big limitation on connectedness. It doesn't mean that our various systems aren't connected. It just means they aren't so densely interconnected as the Extreme Connectedness Assumption says they are.

A second pervasive feature is *redundancy*. Humans, like other organisms, often have backup systems. Like modularity, redundancy is a big advantage—or rather, a must—given the challenges organisms face. Redundancy lessens the worry about unwittingly damaging something else when you try to improve something. Even if you damage something, the results may not be so bad, when there's a backup. Furthermore, redundancy in gene function (having an extra copy of the same gene) allows one of the genes to take on a new function through natural selection. That's another reason we shouldn't be surprised to see redundancy.

Canalization is a third feature that makes the seamless web idea dubious. It's the nifty ability of an organism's developmental processes to create a particular trait in the face of variations in genes or in environmental factors. Different recipes, same dish. In other words, you get the same phenotype across different genetic and environmental backgrounds. That means that the successful development of a particular trait is not as precarious as it would be if there were only one recipe for producing it. The implication for genetic enhancement is clear: You don't always have to get the genetic alteration exactly right to produce the desired effect. Once again, the web isn't so seamless; the interconnectedness isn't so dense.

None of this shows that there isn't a risk of unwittingly disrupting some beneficial connection if we intervene with a biomedical enhancement. But it does show that it's a mistake to assume that we're so densely interconnected that it's always foolish to try to improve ourselves. Sometimes it *will* be foolish, but that will depend on the particulars. We can't simply rule out biomedical enhancement across the board, or even genetic enhancement, with huge generalizations about extreme connectedness and seamless webs.

Social conservatives like Lord Devlin and bioconservatives like Fukuyama and Bush's Council rest their case against attempts to improve the human condition on the Extreme Connectedness Assumption, without providing any evidence to back it up. Even worse, they ignore what evidence there is. There's a good deal of evidence that both individual organisms and societies are pretty resilient and that their resiliency is a function of loose connections. Evolutionary biology explains why organisms couldn't *not* be resilient and how loose connections make for resiliency. If societies, like organisms, face selective pressures and have to respond to changing challenges, then they have to be resilient, too. And if they're to be resilient, then they can't be too densely interconnected. That's why Devlin's prediction of catastrophe was dubious even before events showed it to be false. Some environmentalists make a similar mistake: They simply assume, without looking closely at the facts, that "the environment" is a seamless web, that every species is a "keystone" species whose loss will cause the whole environment to crash. It's simply not true that every species is critical for the functioning of other species. Countless species have gone extinct in the past without such drastic consequences.

Of course, we have to be on the lookout for tight connections that might be disrupted by our enhancement interventions, just as we have to be careful not to destroy features of the environment that really are like the keystone in an arch. That's different from assuming that tight connections are so all-pervasive as to rule out any intervention whatsoever. To know when we're dealing with an area of dense interconnectedness and where we're not, we have to rely on *knowledge about the particular causal relationships that make the organism work*. Later, I'll offer a set of risk-reducing principles that focus on particular causal relationships. They force us to look for master threads that hold the fabric together and avoid snipping them.

One last point about connectedness. There's an important instance of it that creates a lot of mischief in ordinary, unassisted evolution. Fitness-decreasing genes are often located right next to fitness-increasing ones on chromosomes. This means that when the DNA gets shuffled in old-fashioned reproduction, you often get the bad with the good. In other words, "nature" routinely does what bioconservatives fear we'll do with genetic enhancement: produce bad consequences in the process of seeking improvement. This is one more big limitation on unintentional genetic modification I didn't mention in chapter 3. Intentional modification can avoid this problem, by picking out the good genes and leaving the bad ones behind. The moral of this story is that connectedness isn't an obstacle to progress when we can sever the connections.

But Aren't Genetic Changes Irreversible?

Some people who aren't hostile to biomedical enhancements in general draw the line at genetic enhancements. They think genetic enhancements are too risky because they would produce irreversible changes. If we make a mistake, it's uncorrectable and it will be passed on from generation to generation. Irrevocable, self-perpetuating harms are the scariest kind, no doubt.

What does it mean to say that a mistake in a genetic enhancement would be irreversible? To answer this question, we have to distinguish between changing genes and the effects of changing them. Suppose we insert a gene in an embryo. If we do this early enough, then the change gets replicated in every cell in the organism's body, including its sex cells (sperm and eggs). That means that if the organism reproduces, the genetic change may get passed on. Suppose that this change is a big mistake: The gene turns out to be associated with a bad consequence we didn't foresee. Does it follow that we've made an irrevocable error?

No, it doesn't, because genetic changes don't have to mean phenotypic (trait) changes. Whether a genetic change produces a phenotypic change depends on whether the gene gets expressed. Genes don't express automatically. They have to be switched on. We already know how to prevent genes from being expressed. Scientists can insert a gene into a mouse embryo and administer a drug that prevents it from being expressed. They can also alter the gene they insert so that a drug has to be administered to trigger its expression. That means that even if the *genetic change* is permanent and self-replicating across the generations, it doesn't follow that the usual *consequences of having the gene* are. It's the consequences that matter. So, saying that genetic enhancements are irreversible is awfully misleading. Once we appreciate the big gap between genotype and phenotype, genetic enhancement looks a good deal less risky.

There's another point about irreversibility worth pondering. The biggest worry arises in the case of organisms that may escape from our control, that have short generation times, and that are capable of lateral gene transfer. That description applies to genetically applied bacteria, not to genetically modified humans.

Still, this misleading talk about irreversibility gropes toward a genuine concern. If we undertake genetic alterations of any kind— whether as enhancements or to prevent diseases—we need to proceed with great caution. Being cautious means, among other things, trying to limit mistakes, if we are at risk of making them. Later in this chapter, I'll suggest some concrete ways of doing this.

Strategies for Coping with Risk

Biomedical enhancements pose different kinds of risks—biological, social, psychological, maybe moral as well. In the rest of this chapter,

I'm focusing on biological risks. More specifically, I want to think about how we can reduce the biological risks of genetic enhancements. Starting there makes sense, because genetic enhancement is thought to be the riskiest kind. If we can identify conditions where the risks of genetic enhancement would be kept to an acceptable minimum, that would go a long way toward showing that it's a mistake to reject biomedical enhancement generally, on the grounds that it's too risky. Some of what I say about genetic enhancement will apply to other kinds of risks and other modes of enhancement, too.

The goal is to reduce the risks to acceptable levels, not to zero. Eliminating risk isn't possible. Life isn't like that. But even if it were possible, eliminating risk would be a mistake, because the costs of doing this would be too high. The costs include both the benefits we forgo and the costs we bear because of our efforts to eliminate risk.

When thinking about risk, the idea of *the marginal cost of risk reduction* is very important. Here's an example. Suppose we can achieve a 10% reduction of serious injury in a car crash for every additional one-eighth inch of steel we add to the body of a car. If we add enough to make the doors as thick as the hull of an Abrams tank, nobody will die in a car crash (unless they run into an Abrams tank). But beyond a certain point, an additional increment of risk reduction (another one-eighth inch of steel in this case) isn't worth it. The car becomes unaffordable and the cost of gas for such a heavy vehicle becomes prohibitive.

In every other area of life, we tolerate some risk in order to reap benefits and avoid harm. Why should genetic enhancement be any different? And notice: We tolerate risk not just to avoid harms but also to gain benefits. In chapter 6 we'll see that Michael Sandel thinks it's a mistake to think of enhancement, genetic or otherwise, in terms of costs and benefits. We'll also see that he's understanding talk about costs and benefits in an unduly narrow way. For now the point is commonsensical: The goal of genetic enhancement, as with other human activities, is to reduce risk to acceptable levels, where what counts as acceptable depends on what you have to give up to get each additional increment of risk reduction.

There are three basic approaches to the risks of genetic enhancement. You can try to prohibit it altogether. You can try to limit the risk by following a single, general, master risk-reducing principle. Or you can rely on a set of more particular risk-reducing principles. I'm going to try to persuade you that the third approach is best, and I'm actually going to provide a set of risk-reducing principles. First, I have to show that the other two approaches aren't promising.

I've already said a lot that should make you skeptical of prohibition. Back in chapter 1, I noted that enhancements will inevitably continue to come in through the back door with efforts to treat and prevent diseases. We could kill the golden goose because we don't like some of its eggs, but in the case of medical research nobody in their right mind wants to do that. So prohibiting the development of the ability to enhance is a nonstarter.

Trying to prohibit the *use* of enhancements after medical research shows them to be feasible doesn't look promising either. For one thing, if you prohibit biomedical enhancement in the United States or other countries where there's strong regulation of research, you can bet it will go elsewhere. The result won't be prevention of enhancements, it'll be uncontrolled enhancements. For another, it would be very hard to justify an across-the-board ban on enhancements in a democratic country that values liberty and improvement. We celebrate the historic enhancements—literacy, computers, the development of institutions that allow us to live better, etc. How could we ban new enhancements just because they use biomedical means?

Even a ban limited to genetic enhancements seems arbitrary, if this means a permanent ban. We may know enough to say that we shouldn't allow any genetic enhancement of human beings for now, but we don't know enough to rule it out forever. If we continue to become more and more adept at manipulating genes in laboratory animals and if altering our own genes is necessary for our survival or to achieve great benefits, a permanent ban will be hard to justify. Under these conditions, what right would the government have to tell us that we can't use this technology? Why would we vote to have our government tell us that? The answer can't be that genetic enhancements are unnatural or that they interfere with the wisdom of nature or evolution's master engineer or that the human organism is so densely interconnected that we can't ever alter any aspect of it without unacceptable damage. We now know that all that is rubbish.

There might be other, more cogent reasons for a permanent ban on genetic enhancement. We'll consider two of them in chapters 5 and 6, respectively: the worry that genetic enhancements, and perhaps other kinds as well, will worsen social injustices, and Michael Sandel's charge that pursuing enhancements is a sign of bad character and will make our character worse. For now, I only want to emphasize two points. First, prohibition doesn't look realistic, not if the benefits are great enough. To put it crudely, where there's strong demand, you can bet there'll be supply. Second, trying to justify laws permanently prohibiting all genetic enhancements will be—and should be—an uphill battle, at least in a democratic country that values liberty and making our lives better. The more we learn about genetic alterations to prevent disease and the better we get at making genetic enhancements of laboratory animals, the better equipped we'll eventually be to undertake high-value genetic enhancements in humans. If that's how it goes, it's hard to see why we would want a permanent ban on genetic enhancements. The problems with prohibition are serious enough that we should consider the other two alternatives.

The Precautionary Principle

The Precautionary Principle is a single, master principle for reducing risks. Some people invoke it when they oppose genetically modified foods. Some go further and say it forbids any genetic modification of anything, from lab mice to humans. It's hard to evaluate the Precautionary Principle because there's no one official statement of it. The various statements of it that exist are not only ambiguous but also possibly inconsistent with each other. Often, it is understood to put a very strong burden of proof on those who want to engage in some new activity (like genetically modifying food crops) that *might* cause serious harm. The idea is that those who want to prevent the activity or take action to reduce the harm it might cause don't have to show that there's good scientific evidence that the activity is likely to cause the harm before taking action. On a stronger interpretation, the principle also says that those who want to engage in the activity have to provide good scientific evidence that it *won't* cause harm (or serious harm) before they're allowed to act.

The odd thing about the Precautionary Principle in all its formulations is that it doesn't take benefits into account, only harms. In fact, it doesn't even take all harms into account, only those that might be caused by *new* human activities. Think about some of the greatest potential harms we face now. Many of them are the result of human activities we've been engaged in for a while, not new activities. Global warming is one example among many. Suppose someone proposes a new technology for reducing global warming gases. On one interpretation, the Precautionary Principle says that it's permissible to take action to stop this technology from being used if it *might* cause serious harm, even if we don't have good scientific evidence that it is likely to do so. But what if this technology is our only realistic hope of averting a greater harm—the harm that will be caused by the actions we've already taken since the beginning of the industrial revolution? What if we have very good evidence that it will solve the global warming problem and we have good, though not airtight evidence that it would not be very risky? The Precautionary Principle authorizes quashing the technology. That's extreme, and dangerous.

Some people who endorse the Precautionary Principle do so because they have a certain picture of our world. Things are naturally in balance. New human activities, like genetically modifying crops or genetically enhancing human capacities, are likely to throw things out of balance. They assume that new human activities are the real threat. But what about the human activities that contribute to global warming? They aren't new. It seems irrational to say that we can't intervene with new technologies to solve problems that existing technologies have caused, unless we can show with scientific certainty that the new technologies won't cause harm. The real question should be whether the new technologies carry acceptable risks. If the harms they are designed to prevent are great enough—and they surely are in the case of global warming—then we should tolerate more risk. If we follow the Precautionary Principle, we won't be able to correct the problems we've already caused. We won't be able to restore the balance that we've already upset. That's irrational.

The astute environmental philosopher Stephen Gardiner has suggested a way of interpreting the Precautionary Principle that makes it look more reasonable. He says we can think of it as a rule from decision theory, applied to policy choices involving technologies or environmental regulation.

The decision rule in question is called the Maximin Principle. "Maximin" is short for "Maximize the minimum payoff." Here's the idea. Suppose you have to decide between only two options. Option A is going to a local community experimental theatre production. Option B is staying home and watching an HBO series that you like, even though you don't think it's as good as *The Wire*. The worst outcome if you stay home is that the episode tonight is somewhat subpar—not as interesting as the average episode in this series. That outcome isn't so bad, because the series has a reputation for being consistent and it's a pretty good series. The worst outcome if you go to the play will be grim indeed: Few aesthetic experiences are as excruciating as really bad experimental theatre. The Maximin Principle tells you to stay home: to choose the option that has the least bad worst outcome.

Notice that in applying the Maximin Principle to the choice of entertainment you didn't consider the best outcomes of either option, only the worst outcomes. The best outcome in the case of the experimental theatre production might be wonderful—you get to witness the debut of a new, exciting kind of theatre. The best outcome with the HBO series would be one of the better episodes in a series that's good, but nothing special.

Why shouldn't we consider the best outcomes as well as the worst in making the decision? The answer is that we should, unless we're abjectly fearful. The Maximin Principle only makes sense if you are literally obsessed with avoiding the worst outcome and care absolutely nothing about benefits. In decision theory terms, the Maximin Principle is for those who have infinite risk-aversion.

There's another limitation on the Maximin Principle. It's appropriate for decisions under uncertainty, not decisions under risk. In a decision under risk, you know what the possible outcomes of the various options are and you can attach some probability to their occurring (where the probability is greater than zero and less than one, i.e., a sure thing). In decision-making under uncertainty, your ignorance is staggering: You don't know the probabilities of the possible outcomes.

If you knew the probabilities of the outcomes—if you were making a decision under risk, rather than uncertainty—you could simply calculate the expected payoffs for each of the options. You would do this by multiplying the probability of each outcome times the magnitude of the payoff for that outcome (the net benefit you'd get if that outcome were realized—the benefits minus the costs). Then you would just choose the option with the highest expected payoff.

The moral of this excursion into decision theory is that if you think of the Precautionary Principle as the Maximin Principle applied to policy choices about things like genetically modified foods or genetic enhancements of humans, it only makes sense if two very demanding conditions are satisfied. First, we have to care nothing about the possible benefits of the technology and be concerned only about avoiding the worst-case scenario if we use it. Second, we have to be nearly totally ignorant about how probable the effects of using the technology are.

Neither of these conditions is satisfied in all cases of genetic enhancement. We care about benefits, not just harms. Some genetic enhancements may be extremely valuable, either in terms of improving our condition relative to the status quo, or for helping preserve the status quo. And we're not in a state of total ignorance. We have a lot of knowledge about the effects of genetic alterations in animals that are very similar to us biologically. In fact, scientists have already succeeded in making a number of genetic enhancements in mice. Genes have been inserted that make mice much stronger, give them more stamina for physical tasks, and improve their maze-running smarts. To get an idea of how fast mouse-enhancement progress is occurring, consult Anders Sandberg's website, "Anders's Top Ten Genetic Enhancements"—he has to constantly update it. (Sandberg is a multifaceted genius—a philosopher, neuroscientist, futurist, mathematician, and computer graphics artist who works at the Uehiro Centre for Practical Ethics at Oxford.) A quick look at Anders's list indicates that the postmouse future will arrive considerably ahead of the post-human future, and that's a good thing. Let them be the risk-pioneers. We share a lot of genes in common with mice. So as our knowledge of the effects of genetic enhancements in mice grows, we move farther away from the home turf of the Maximin Principle.

We also have a substantial and increasing fund of more direct knowledge about how various genes work in humans. Some of this we get from seeing what happens when some humans lack the gene in question; some we get from observing the effects that variations of a particular gene have on phenotype. In the case of many particular genetic alterations, we already have a basis for making reasonable probability estimates of the outcomes and this knowledge will only increase over time.

This doesn't mean that we now have enough knowledge to go ahead with genetic enhancements in humans. But it does mean that the near total ignorance condition isn't satisfied and that we are leaving it farther behind with every passing day. Because we aren't in a state of near total ignorance and we do care about benefits, not just about avoiding the worst harms, then we ought to reject the Precautionary Principle on its Maximin interpretation. It's not a good guide for evaluating the risk of genetic enhancements.

The Precautionary Principle is the most famous example of a single, master principle for risk reduction in making choices about technologies. There may be others worth considering, but I can't think of any. I'm not terribly worried that I've overlooked one, because

I suspect that a single, master principle would be too good to be true. I see no reason to think there's a risk-reduction magic bullet.

We need a more fine-grained approach, one that doesn't lump all enhancements, or even all genetic enhancements, together. We'll need a set of risk-reduction principles, not just one. They should take into account the extent of our knowledge and how it varies from enhancement to enhancement. They should reflect the fact that our knowledge is rapidly increasing. They should focus on the fact that genetic enhancement is an intervention at the beginning of the process of human development. That means they should focus on how to reduce the risk of throwing a wrench into the developmental process. To do that, our precautionary principles will have to be informed by the best scientific knowledge of how that process works. Finally, they should help us limit the damage if we make a mistake. Here's a set of principles that satisfy these criteria.

Risk-Reduction Rules of Thumb

The following items are what the famous philosopher John Rawls called "counting principles." The idea is that the more of them that are satisfied and the more fully each of them is satisfied, the more confident we should be that we've covered the bases in trying to reduce the risk of bad unintended consequences. They aren't intended as a foolproof method of eliminating risk. We've seen that we shouldn't hanker after that anyway. Remember, they're intended for a very specific task: reducing the risk of unintended bad biological consequences in the case of genetic enhancements. They're appropriate for genetic modifications generally, however. They make sense regardless of whether the modifications are intended to enhance normal capacities or to prevent diseases. In either case, what we have to worry about is unwittingly doing something to a gene that will disrupt the developmental process that begins with the embryo. That's why they focus on what biologists call *ontogenic causal relationships*—the chains of causes and effects that occur as the organism's development unfolds. They're formulated in terms that apply to other organisms, not just humans, because they rely on general facts about ontogeny, the developmental process.

1. The intervention targets genes at shallower ontogenic depths. Or, to use a different aquatic metaphor, genes that get switched on further downstream in the developmental cascade. This makes sense, because the consequences of a mistake in the case of a gene that does its work "upstream" in the process, nearer the beginning, is likely to have greater ill effects. Upstream errors have a cascading effect, so, other things being equal, we should avoid interventions upstream.

2. The intervention, if successful, wouldn't produce an enhancement that exceeds the upper limit of the current normal distribution of the trait in question. Suppose the trait is intelligence as measured by IQ tests. If some people already have IQs of 140, and it looks like they're doing okay, then we're on safer ground making a genetic change that will result in an individual who would have had an IQ of 120 having one of 140 than we would be in making a change that results in an individual with an IQ of 240, which is higher than anybody has ever had. Once we get beyond the top end of the normal range, we're in uncharted waters. So, other things being equal, it's safer to stay within the current normal range. Using this principle as a rule of thumb is compatible with allowing exceptions in extreme cases. Some gains above normal could be so important that they're worth pursuing. That might be the case, for example, if we needed to

engineer much more effective immune systems to reduce the ravages of old age or to fend off emerging pandemics. Another example where it might be reasonable to enhance beyond the top of the current normal range would be a cognitive enhancement that helped us solve problems that seem intractable given our current limitations.

3. The intervention's effects are limited to the organism. This is important, but relatively easy to accomplish in the case of mammals like us. One of the big worries about genetically modified crops is that modified seeds can escape from experimental plots. Fortunately, human sperm, eggs, and embryos aren't like that. They don't get blown around by the wind, and they can't hitchhike on the fur of passing animals or in the digestive systems of birds. As I already noted, we already have techniques for switching genes off or engineering them so that they have to be switched on with a special chemical. So, we're already on our way toward developing good containment techniques that prevent bad effects from being passed on to future generations. (Remember, whether the genes get passed on doesn't matter as such; it's the effects of the expression of the genes that counts.) This guideline also obviously speaks in favor of small-scale applications of genetic enhancements, limited to a few individuals at first.

4. The intervention's effects stay compartmentalized within the organism. In other words, the intervention modifies a highly modularized system or subsystem. This reduces the chance of unintended spillover effects.

5. The intervention's effects are reversible. If this condition is satisfied, ongoing damage can be avoided. Reversing bad unintended effects could be accomplished in a number of different ways: Drugs that counteract the effects of gene expression or stop the gene from expressing in the first place are the two most obvious.

6. The intervention shouldn't result in major morphological changes—big alterations in the basic design and shape of the organism. *Organisms aren't like seamless webs, but they aren't like Legos or Mr. Potato Head either.* We should avoid genetic alterations that would be likely to produce changes in the basic architecture of the organism.

7. If the goal of the genetic alteration is to eliminate some undesirable trait, then both the causal role of that trait in the life of the organism *and* the functions of the genes that are changed to eliminate the trait should be well understood. The idea here is that both traits and the genes that underlie them can have multiple roles to play. We want to avoid throwing out the baby with the bathwater: eliminating a gene because it plays a role in a bad trait but failing to see that it also makes a necessary contribution to a good trait; or failing to see that a "bad" trait is only bad in some respects, but valuable in others.

This list isn't meant to be comprehensive. It's a good start, but it needs refining and supplementing as well. My main purpose is to show what a more fine-grained approach to risk-reduction would look like. I also hope to stimulate a more fruitful discussion. It's time to get beyond two extreme, equally unhelpful responses to the problem of unintended consequences: on the one hand, declaring that we shouldn't undertake any genetic enhancements ever because we'll destroy the work of the master engineer or unravel the seamless web; on the other hand, muttering vagaries about proceeding with caution, without explaining what that means in concrete terms.

These risk-reducing rules of thumb have the advantage of being knowledge-sensitive. They focus on what we need to know to make prudent choices regarding genetic enhancement, and they make room for advances in knowledge. In fact, they even provide guidance for what sort of knowledge we should try to gain. More specifically, they focus our attention on what counts when it comes to genetic enhancement, or genetic alteration of any kind: the causal relationships involved in ontogeny, the process of development that begins with the embryo.

At this point, we simply don't know enough to attempt even a small-scale experiment in genetic enhancement for humans. We don't know enough about the relevant causal relationships. Because they focus on causal relationships, these seven rules force us to face up to that. But at the same time, they are designed to take into account the fact that our knowledge is growing and that at some point we may be in a position to undertake responsible genetic enhancements.

Conclusion

My aims in this chapter have been pretty modest. I haven't tried to make the case that we should undertake any biomedical enhancements, much less that we should plunge into genetically engineering human embryos. Mainly, I've tried to clear up some confusions in how we tend to think about the risk of unintended bad consequences when it comes to biomedical enhancements. A good deal of the confusion stems from faulty analogies—master engineers, seamless webs, and so on. The problem with these analogies is that they don't fit what we know about biology since the Darwinian revolution. If we continue to think about ourselves and nature the way people did before Darwin came on the scene, we'll have a distorted view of the risks of enhancement. We'll jump to the conclusion that all genetic enhancement and maybe other biomedical enhancements as well are too risky. Another confusion has to do with the supposed irreversibility of genetic changes. It doesn't matter whether genetic changes are irreversible; what matters is whether their effects are avoidable. We already know how to avoid irrevocable, self-replicating mistakes by switching off genes or counteracting their effects.

In this chapter and the preceding one, I've said quite a lot about biomedical enhancements that involve changing the genes that will be passed on to the next generation. But it is vitally important to remember that some of the most valuable biomedical enhancements may not involve genetic modification. This is worth bearing in mind, because it means that even if genetic enhancements are too risky—at least for the foreseeable future—it doesn't follow that biomedical enhancement should be off the table. One of the most exciting developments in biology in recent years is the field of epigenetics, which studies the ways in which chemicals in the environment—including the uterine environment in which the fetus develops—can change the expression of genes. As Dr. Sharon Moalem puts it, we now know that genes are not rigid blueprints. Without changing genes, we can modify their expression, creating new traits that we previously thought could only be produced by the more radical techniques of genetic engineering. So, even if you have serious reservations about genetic enhancements, you should still keep an open mind about other modes of enhancement. My hunch is that widespread genetic enhancements of humans will not occur for a long time, if ever.

In this chapter, I've repeatedly emphasized the importance of focusing on the facts about evolution. That's absolutely necessary for two reasons. First, it shows us just how flawed we are and how mistaken it would be to assume that if we don't enhance, things will be just fine. Second, it provides guidance for developing reasonable approaches to evaluating the risks of biomedical enhancements and for taking reasonable steps to reduce them.

One final caveat is in order. I've only compared intentional genetic modification for purposes of enhancement with ordinary evolution as usual when they are regarded as tools or techniques for improving or sustaining human life. I've argued that UGM is in several respects a defective tool—that there are serious limitations on its effectiveness and efficiency as a device for making our lives better and even for sustaining our current level of well-being. And I've also argued that in principle IGM could do a better job. I wanted to do this in order to combat a common prejudice against IGM, a negative attitude based on an overly rosy—and grossly inaccurate—understanding of evolution as usual.

The "in principle" warrants strong emphasis. Even if IGM is a better tool, it doesn't follow that we should use it. There is, after all, such a thing as user-error. Even if IGM has the potential to make our lives better and to preserve us in the face of threats to our survival, we might not be capable of using this tool safely. I'm convinced that at present we aren't capable of using it safely on human beings. My point is that, given how great the potential of this tool is, we should think hard about how to use it safely, rather than taking it off the table permanently. The reason for refraining from IGM (at least for now) is our own fallibility, not the infallibility of mother nature.

In this chapter I've only focused on the biological harms we might unwittingly cause by genetic enhancements. In the next two chapters, I address other worries.

5 | WILL THE RICH GET BIOLOGICALLY RICHER?

Remember Michelle and Carlos? They grew up and apart. Michelle became psychologically dependent on Ritalin. She became convinced that she couldn't think well without it. When she didn't take it, her lack of self-confidence impaired her ability to focus, and that reinforced her belief that she had to have it. She hated feeling drug-dependent and finally went cold turkey. Michelle's experience with Ritalin dampened her enthusiasm for biomedical enhancements in general.

Carlos moved in the opposite direction. After graduation, he went into business with his father, but after five years he decided to go to law school. He quit smoking for health reasons but found that caffeine wasn't enough to sustain his attention while plowing through dull cases. So in 2015 he began taking the first FDA-approved enhancement drug. Carlos's enhancement drug, unlike Michelle's, came through the front door, and he was completely satisfied with its effects. Carlos became a corporate lawyer. Michelle became a social worker specializing in the treatment of drug dependency. Carlos got rich; Michelle didn't.

Fast forward a generation. By an ironic coincidence, Michelle's daughter and Carlos's son are competing for the same middle-management position in a big corporation. Carlos II gets the job.

Because she has a friend in the personnel department, Michelle II finds out that he got it because his application included a "Certificate of Enhancement" from Bioboost, Inc., a company that tailors a complex cocktail of enhancement drugs to the customer's individual genome. According to Bioboost's advertisements, people who have the benefit of their product are smarter, less prone to depression, and miss fewer work days due to illness.

Some people in the scientific community think that Bioboost's marketing campaign exaggerates the effectiveness of its product. Big corporations are aware of this, but they think the evidence is strong enough to show that Bioboost customers have an edge, other things being equal. In the case of Michelle II and Carlos II, other things were equal, so being Bioboosted was the tiebreaker.

Does Michelle II have grounds for complaint? Is she a victim of discrimination in hiring? Is it wrong for people who use biomedical enhancements to reap greater economic rewards? Does it matter whether the enhancements are very expensive? Is her predicament like that of a "clean" athlete who loses a race to a competitor who took a performance-enhancing drug?

Michelle II might not have been able to afford Bioboost (her mom is a social worker). But even if she could, she might have had scruples about this particular enhancement or enhancements generally. (That wouldn't be surprising, given her mother's bad experience with an earlier enhancement drug.) Should she be economically penalized for her reservations about enhancement? Maybe Carlos II had scruples, too; maybe his desire to get the job overpowered them.

Carlos II *says* he doesn't see a problem. What if the Bioboost package is so expensive that some otherwise qualified candidates can't afford it? That's true of tuition at the best colleges and law schools as well. Yes, it's true that he could afford Bioboost because his family is rich. Yes, that means that he doesn't *merit* the advantages that Bioboost gives him. They are *unearned* advantages. But the same is true of the higher-than-average IQ that he would still have if he didn't take Bioboost. He didn't earn that either. IQ gets established pretty early in life, largely as a result of genetic and environmental factors beyond the individual's control. So, what's the problem? Why single out enhancement drugs as undeserved advantages? Life is riddled with unearned advantages.

Losing out on a job she really wanted to a Bioboooster has concentrated Michelle II's mind on fairness issues. "Yes, it's true that life's riddled with unearned advantages," she says. "But that's no reason to make it worse than it is. The fact that injustices already exist doesn't excuse new injustices. We shouldn't be developing technologies that we know will increase unfairness. We make athletes undergo urine tests to see if they've cheated by using performance enhancement drugs. We ought to do the same for job applicants."

Carlos II and Michelle II are both wrong. He's wrong for the reason she cites: The fact that unfair advantages already exist doesn't justify tolerating new ones. Some unfair advantages shouldn't be tolerated. That's the rationale behind making sure that every child has a basic education, even if his parents can't afford it. It's also the reason why we ought to pay for repairing a child's crippling congenital hip deformity or club foot, if the parents can't pay for it. But Michelle II is wrong to suggest that the mere fact that a technology will cause unearned advantages is a sufficient reason to try to prevent its development, and she's naïve to assume that we will be able to prevent biomedical enhancements. She's also making a more profound mistake: thinking that every unearned advantage is an injustice. In any world where chance plays a role, there will be unearned advantages.

Now fast-forward three more generations. Some job applicants have a *genetic* enhancement certificate; others don't. The genetic enhancement certificate states that the embryo from which the person developed was engineered for improvement, by the insertion of genes that increase the probability the person will have certain desirable traits. The situation isn't like that portrayed in the film *Gattaca*: There's no official social policy of excluding the unenhanced from various occupations. Nonetheless, there's a marked tendency on the part of private employers to favor genetic enhancement, at least as a tiebreaker. The genetically enhanced aren't like a different species, and it's not possible for prospective parents to "design" their children. (Remember: Our genes are just part of what makes us who we are. You can design the genotype of an embryo, but you can't design a child.) But if parents opt for genetic enhancement, their children will tend to have higher-than-average IQs, fewer sick days, and fewer psychological problems, including depression. The genetically enhanced also tend to live somewhat longer.

Before we go any further pondering these possibilities, I want to emphasize a simple point. We already live in a world where some are enhanced and some aren't. Most children born in affluent countries have higher IQs, fewer sick days, fewer psychological problems, and *much* longer lives than most children born in the "less-developed" countries. It's not just the countries that are "less-developed"; it's the people as well. They are often malnourished during gestation and throughout their whole lives, infected with debilitating parasites, stunted in their physical and neurological development. Not surprisingly, they are also at higher risk for mental illnesses. Think of it as a heartless social lottery: Whether you live or die or live well or miserably depends in great part on the kind of society you happen to be born into.

An unblinking view of such gross unfairness is simply too much for some people to bear. They either avert their eyes or, if they're traditional Hindus, embrace the doctrine of karma. The losers in the social lottery aren't really the victims of blind chance. They're paying for sins committed in former lives.

We already have a morally arbitrary allocation of genes, without genetic enhancement. In other words, there's a natural lottery as well as a social lottery. Some people win big in the natural lottery—they get a better overall packet of genes. In fact, genetic enhancement techniques may never produce gaps as large as the ones that exist now as the result of the combined social-natural lottery we all participate in. This doesn't mean that genetic enhancement isn't problematic, only that it's not uniquely problematic or morally novel.

Focusing on Unjust Inequalities

We're entering the most hotly contested neighborhood in the war zone of political disagreement: the dispute over the relationship between inequality and justice. The sources of disagreement aren't just political; they reach down to the deepest levels of a twenty-five-hundred-year-old argument about the nature of justice. In spite of all the disagreement, there's convergence on a simple point that often gets lost in the debate about biomedical enhancements: Not all inequalities are unjust. This means, for starters, that the mere fact that some people have access to biomedical enhancements and some don't isn't an argument against enhancement. The trick is to try to develop a reasonable, and reasonably wide, consensus on *which* sorts of inequalities, under which conditions, we ought to be really worried about.

We need such a consensus if we're to develop a coherent social policy response to biomedical enhancements. Yet a consensus on what's just and what isn't seems to be beyond our reach. In the United States, there's fierce and apparently intractable disagreement between liberals and conservatives on whether justice requires a legally recognized right to health care for all citizens and on much else as well. There's an astounding amount of disagreement on issues much less difficult than justice, too. Americans can't even agree on whether the earth was created more than ten thousand years ago (30% say it wasn't). Given that we can't even agree on the facts, how can we hope to agree on justice? When we look beyond our borders to countries with quite different traditions and cultures, the prospects for agreement about justice seem even slimmer.

I want to sketch a view about the relationship between justice and equality that could provide a starting point for developing a working consensus on how to respond to the challenge of biomedical enhancements. I'm probably too optimistic in hoping it could eventually be developed into a working consensus. But even if we never come to a working consensus, each of us will be forced to take a stand on the justice issue as biomedical enhancements become an increasingly important fact of life. Perhaps my sketch will be of help to some of you.

My approach rejects the assumption that inequality in the distribution of biomedical enhancements is in itself an injustice. It then focuses on two possible effects of some people not having access to biomedical enhancements: domination and exclusion.

Domination occurs when inequalities in goods (income, wealth, education, biomedical enhancements) result in some people being able to exert excessive control over others, levels of control that create opportunities for systematic exploitation and other serious forms of injustice. The primary example is political domination. If some people have so much more wealth than others that they are able to manipulate the political process, then democracy becomes a sham. The government is no longer the agent of the people; it's merely a tool—or a weapon—by which some people exercise power over the rest.

In our world, for better or worse, governments are very powerful. So inequalities in goods that are severe enough to result in some people controlling the government have a multiplying effect. When one group becomes politically dominant it can use the awesome power of the state to become dominant in all areas of social life. The political domination that extreme inequalities in wealth creates is itself an injustice—a violation of the right to democratic government. But this injustice inevitably leads to others: economic exploitation, cronyism, partiality in the administration of justice, every form of corruption. Because of this injustice-multiplying effect, we should be especially concerned about inequalities in access to biomedical enhancements that are likely to promote political domination. That's one kind of inequality that is clearly unjust. We should be able to agree on that even if we disagree about whether some other inequalities are unjust.

If one group gains control of the government, it often exercises this power to dominate by excluding certain groups from various benefits. They may be excluded from the basic protections all citizens are supposed to enjoy. In extreme cases, certain people are declared enemies, or even nonpersons, rounded up, shot, gassed, or hacked to pieces. But people can suffer exclusion without this being the deliberate aim of government policy, and exclusion can occur without bloodshed. People can be excluded from sheer neglect, if they lack the resources to participate in mainstream society.

The work of the Nobel Prize–winning economist and philosopher Amartya Sen documents the fact that hundreds of millions of people in less-developed countries are excluded from effective participation in the emerging global economy. We've already met them: Mentally and physically compromised by disease and material deprivation, and too poor to afford to become literate, they are relegated to grueling, often dangerous manual labor, with no possibility for improving their condition. Often they're too weak to work at all before they even reach what you and I consider early middle age.

People who are concerned about justice often quote figures showing that inequality in wealth has vastly increased in the last fifty years. But it isn't really inequality per se that matters. What matters is domination and exclusion—and *deprivation*. By deprivation, I mean extreme poverty, extreme ill health, and powerlessness. Inequality is a matter of how well off you are relative to others. You may be a lot less well off than some others, but that's not necessarily a concern if you are well *enough* off—that is, you aren't suffering deprivation. Even if you are not suffering deprivation—you have enough food, shelter, etc., to live a reasonably comfortable life—you may still suffer domination. But here, too, what matters is not inequality per se, but the fact that if inequalities in wealth become great enough, some people will dominate others in almost every sphere of social life, and some people will be excluded from long-term, effective participation in the mainstream economy.

The same is true for inequalities in access to biomedical enhancements. We shouldn't be any more worried about inequalities per se here than we are with other goods. We should focus instead on the question of whether unequal access to some biomedical enhancements will promote domination and exclusion—and on whether access to enhancements can lift people out of a condition of deprivation.

Earlier, I noted that literacy is a powerful cognitive enhancement. In the modern world, illiterate people are vulnerable to domination. They are more likely to be taken advantage of in a world in which much business is done through written contracts. They are less likely to be able to exercise any of their civil and political rights effectively. They are also likely to have little political influence. Being illiterate also increasingly excludes a person from gainful employment and certainly from jobs that offer much prospect for advancement. Biomedical cognitive enhancements might turn out to be just as vital for human flourishing as literacy has come to be.

As recently as 150 years ago, literacy was a privilege of the minority. In some parts of the world, it still is. Illiteracy is currently at 32% in India and 46% in Pakistan, and in some parts of these countries the majority of people are illiterate.

What's true of literacy is true of the other great historical enhancements—the agrarian revolution, the growth of institutions, computers, and the Internet: They start out as the property of a minority and then diffuse more widely. When it comes to biomedical enhancements, some people seem to forget this basic fact. They are so worried about the unfairness of some people lacking access to biomedical enhancements that they actually propose not developing them or at least not allowing anybody to have them until everybody can! Call this the Equality or Nothing View.

Anyone who holds the Equality or Nothing View is faced with an unsavory choice: They either have to make the same bizarre claim about technologies generally, including the great historical enhancements, or they have to show that biomedical enhancements are radically different from all other technologies. The second alternative looks unpromising for reasons I've already explained: The mere fact that an enhancement involves biotechnology doesn't make a moral difference. The first alternative will also be a hard row to hoe, for reasons I've already explained. I certainly wouldn't want to prevent anyone from having beneficial technologies until everyone could have them. Would you?

Like it or not, technologies always start somewhere and spread; they don't leap full-blown into the world simultaneously at every location. If that's so, then what does the Equality or Nothing View require us to do? Is the idea that if a beneficial technology happens to originate in one locale, we should quarantine it until we reach the point that everybody can have it? That advice is both impractical and morally reprehensible. Impractical, because it's been tried and failed before. (For example, in the eighteenth century the British government tried to prevent people capable of building and maintaining power looms from emigrating, but it didn't work.) Morally reprehensible, because if it could be done it would mean depriving millions of people of something of great value, certainly for decades and maybe forever.

Here's a concrete example to drive home the last point. In rural India, extremely poor women have used cell phones to grow small businesses that they've been able to fund by "micro-financing" offered to them by NGOs. Surely, no one in their right mind would say that these women shouldn't be allowed to use this combination of cognitive and economic enhancement technologies until all the world's poor have access to them. Yet that's precisely what some people who claim to care about justice are saying about biomedical enhancements. Once again, we see the tendency to be dazzled by the adjective "biomedical." We leave our common sense behind when we think about justice and biomedical enhancements. As we've already seen, biomedical enhancements aren't necessarily more powerful than other technologies and they are no more "unnatural" than other human interventions.

So where do we stand in the discussion so far? Because we think that biomedical enhancements may be very beneficial, we worry about whether everyone will have access to them. But the right conclusion to draw is not that we shouldn't let anyone have them until everyone can. Instead, it's that we should try to ensure that the most beneficial enhancements diffuse rapidly. And, we should be especially vigilant about those enhancements that are likely to facilitate domination or the lack of which are likely to cause people to be excluded from productive economic activity. For those, rapid diffusion is a moral necessity. The same is true for biomedical enhancements that would relieve deprivation.

Who is going to help ensure that beneficial biomedical enhancements diffuse rapidly? And how is rapid diffusion to be achieved? To answer these questions, we have to look more closely at what sorts of goods biomedical enhancements are likely to be and how they are likely to be produced and distributed. To do that, once again we'll need to clear up some misconceptions that have hamstrung the debate about biomedical enhancements, especially, the controversy about their likely impact on justice. This will be yet another instance of what I call "epistemic excavation": working down through the layers of rhetoric to expose our unexamined assumptions. ("Epistemic" means "having to do with belief or knowledge.") One item that is high on an epistemic excavator's to-do list is *framing assumptions*.

There are four widely held beliefs that frame much of the discussion about justice and enhancement. Taken together, these assumptions act like the frame of a window looking out on a broad landscape. If you are enthralled by the landscape, you don't even notice the window frame. But the window frame determines how much of the landscape you can see; it may exclude some important items from view altogether. You can't begin to ask whether the frame is obscuring something important until you see that there is a frame between you and what you are trying to see. If our framing assumptions are sufficiently flawed, they not only obscure part of the view; they act more like a distorting lens. Mole hills look like mountains and vice versa.

The first framing assumption is that biomedical enhancements are *personal goods* and that they are *zero-sum*. A personal good is one that benefits only the individual who has it. A good is zero-sum if my having it comes at your expense—my gain is your loss. The classic case of a zero-sum situation is the division of a cake. If I take a large piece, then that amount is subtracted from your share. If we add up all the gains and losses of different individuals in a zero-sum situation, we get zero: The gains exactly balance the losses. Suppose that the only thing you can do with your shares of the cake is eat them and that nobody else is going to benefit from your eating them. Then we have a zero-sum situation with personal goods.

The second framing assumption is that biomedical enhancements will be *market goods*. They'll be produced for profit and marketed, like other consumer goods. The third assumption is that they will be *expensive* market goods. The fourth assumption is that because they will be market goods, the only role for the government will be that of regulating the market. In other words, government won't have a stake in the diffusion of biomedical enhancements. It will regulate them for safety and perhaps require proof of efficacy, as it does with drugs, and it might also require an informed consent process before we're allowed to use them.

If we buy into all four assumptions, then we will have a particular take on the justice issues. We'll be very worried about inequalities in access to biomedical enhancements. The landscape we see will be pretty disturbing: The better-off will purchase goods that will benefit them to the disadvantage of those who can't afford them, and government will be doing nothing to address these troubling inequalities.

All four assumptions are flawed. Many biomedical enhancements won't be personal goods: The benefits that flow from them won't be limited to the persons possessing them. In many cases they will be positive-sum: I'll gain from your having an enhancement, even if I don't have it myself. Furthermore, if I have an enhancement it will be more valuable to me if lots of others have it as well. If lots of people are enhanced, we'll all reap benefits that don't reduce to the sum total of the benefits that the enhanced get from being enhanced. Nor can we assume that biomedical enhancements will be purely market goods: Governments will have powerful reasons for treating some of them as *public* goods and will take steps to ensure that they are developed and made widely available. Let's work through each of these points, using concrete illustrations.

Life Isn't a Competition

First, the zero-sum assumption. I think people uncritically assume that biomedical enhancements will be zero-sum goods because they're mesmerized by one very special enhancement context: performance-enhancing drugs in sports. Life has its competitive moments, but it isn't a game. If you get worried every time you encounter a person who is smarter or stronger or better looking than you are, you're not a person with a well-developed sense of justice; you're afflicted with the vice of envy. Or you're paranoid. Or incredibly insecure.

I'm very happy that there are lots of philosophers who are more creative and insightful than I am. I'm also glad that there are people who are better at math and singing and building things than I am. For the most part, we benefit from others having capacities that are "enhanced" relative to our own. Thankfully, zero-sum encounters are the exception, not the rule.

There are extreme circumstances in which this is not true, of course. If you have the misfortune to live in a failed state like the Democratic Republic of Congo, where the rule of law has broken down, or find yourself in a lifeboat where the food has run out, you should be very worried about people who are stronger or wilier than you. In those circumstances, encounters are likely to be zero-sum. But thankfully that is not the situation most readers of this book are in.

In a decently organized society, things are arranged so that we generally benefit from differences in capacities. Most of the good things we enjoy are the result of a division of labor. We could have a division of labor even if there were no differences in people's capacities, but it wouldn't be as productive. To imagine what this would be like, picture a society in which who was a doctor or a lawyer or a mechanic was determined by a lottery. There wouldn't be any correlation between jobs and capacities. That arrangement would be better than having no division of labor at all, perhaps. But it wouldn't be nearly as productive as one based on differences in capacities.

So, differences in capacities are not necessarily, or even usually, a bad thing. Nor are they necessarily unjust. Yet most differences in capacities have a large undeserved element—they're strongly influenced by the combined natural and social lotteries. That means that if there's something wrong with some people having access to enhancements and others not, it can't be that it's because there would be unearned differences in capacities. I've already suggested what is wrong, when there is something wrong: If the differences are great enough, the unenhanced will be vulnerable to domination and exclusion. That's a problem about extreme inequalities generally, not a special problem for an unequal distribution of biomedical enhancements. And it's a problem we should be doing something about, right across the board, for all valuable technologies.

We ought to be developing two capacities. First, we need to learn how to monitor emerging technologies, in order to determine when they're diffusing so slowly as to create a risk of domination or exclusion. Second, we need to devise ways to speed up diffusion to reduce the risk of domination and exclusion and to alleviate deprivation. A little later on, I'll consider a practical proposal for doing this.

For now, I want to dig a little deeper into this crucial question of what sort of goods biomedical enhancements are likely to be. I want to show what's wrong with the assumption that biomedical enhancements will be personal goods and that access to them will be left to the market.

Network Effects and Positive Externalities

A personal good is one whose benefit accrues solely to the possessor. In a reasonably well-organized society, most enhancements won't be like that. Consider cognitive enhancements. Remember, literacy and computers are among the most powerful nonbiomedical cognitive enhancements. Being literate and being able to use a computer bring direct benefits to those who have these abilities. In most situations, these direct benefits aren't zero-sum: We needn't worry that every time somebody learns to read, somebody is made that much worse off. Literacy and computing also have what economists call *network effects*: The benefit you get from being literate or from being able to use a computer actually increases as more people have these enhancements. In a zero-sum situation, you have to be worried about others getting something valuable, because what they gain you lose. Where there are network effects you have an interest in making sure that others have access to the good, because that makes you better off.

There's no reason to think that biomedical cognitive enhancements will be any different from the traditional, nonbiomedical cognitive enhancements. Suppose lots of people take a safe and effective cognitive enhancement drug. There will be benefits of two kinds, and each will increase as more people get this cognitive enhancement. First, there will be the instrumental benefits: A big pool of cognitively enhanced people will be able to achieve things together that couldn't otherwise be achieved. This happens every day on the Internet, one of our most impressive cognitive enhancements to date. Here's only one recent example. In 2007 a Kenyan lawyer named Ory Okolloh used her blog to suggest the idea of an Internet mapping tool to enable people to report the locations of episodes of political violence—and to do so anonymously. People with the relevant technical skills saw the posting and created the Ushahidi Web platform that can be used by people who lack computers, so long as they have cell phones. In Swahili *ushahidi* means testimony.

There are two things to notice about this brilliant invention. First, the benefits it achieves—in particular greater government accountability—accrue not just to those who have the enhancement we call computer access, but to everybody who is a potential victim of government violence. Second, the more people participate in the Ushahidi Web, the greater the benefits. This cognitive enhancement isn't a personal good, it's far from zero-sum (except for repressive governments), and it's free.

Ushahidi is a *collective* cognitive enhancement that piggybacks on thousands of individual enhancements in the form of computer and cell phone access. Science is a grander example of collective cognitive enhancement. Each individual scientist is cognitively enhanced through a long and demanding period of education and training. But scientific knowledge is not simply the sum of the knowledge of all the scientists working independently. The expertise of individual scientists is employed in a set of practices that define the community of scientists. This community is not only international; it's also intergenerational. Taken together, the scientific community's practices for knowledge-seeking constitute a brilliant collective cognitive enhancement.

Ushahidi and science are good examples of how cognitive enhancements in individuals can be organized to achieve collective cognitive enhancements that are instrumentally valuable, that is, valuable because they are effective means to ends we value. In the Ushahidi case the individual cognitive enhancement is computer and cell phone access; with science it is specialized education and training. Ushahidi is an effective means toward the goal of political accountability; science is an effective means for combating and preventing disease, developing valuable technologies, etc.

If we buy into the assumption that biomedical enhancements will be personal goods—that the benefits they bring will only accrue to the possessors—we miss out on all this. We fail to see that biomedical cognitive enhancements, like cognitive enhancements generally, will bring large-scale social goods.

It's not just cognitive biomedical enhancements that fit this pattern. There are lots of other biomedical enhancements that won't be mere personal goods either. Any enhancement that increases human productivity will tend to have network effects, because if more people are individually more productive, they will be able to work together more productively. We already see this result with vaccination programs and other public health measures: Most human activity is cooperative, and the healthier individuals are, the more they can achieve together. A biomedical enhancement that ramped up the capacities of our immune systems would confer health benefits on each individual, but the total benefit of this enhancement would exceed the sum total of the individual *health* benefits.

In the past, increases in productivity have been the platform for increases in human well-being. All the historical nonbiomedical enhancements—the agrarian revolution, literacy, computers, science—fit this pattern. Increased productivity doesn't ensure increased well-being, but it creates the potential for it. It does this in a number of ways. Increased productivity creates opportunities for more people to escape from unrewarding toil, to have more time for activities other than making a living, and it produces new goods and services while lowering costs. Before humans developed the nutritional enhancement we call cooking, they had to spend a lot of time chewing large amounts of food. With the predigestion that cooking provides, they gained more time for other, more enjoyable and rewarding activities. At the dawn of the agrarian revolution ten thousand years ago, increased productivity was largely a matter of learning to use draft animals and plant crops. Today, at least in countries that have decent government and a functioning economy, it's mainly a matter of improving cognitive skills.

Successful cooperation requires more than cognitive skills. It requires emotional skills and the right sort of motivation as well. Most forms of cooperation require trust and empathy and perseverance. There's evidence from experimental psychology that more intelligent people are better cooperators in some contexts. Individuals who were not only cognitively enhanced, but who also were enhanced in the emotional skills and motivation that are critical for cooperation, might be capable of much more complex and productive forms of cooperation than we have mastered so far.

In deciding whether we should develop new cognitive enhancements, instrumental value is important. But cognitive enhancements are also *intrinsically* valuable: Most people enjoy knowledge just for the sake of knowing, and many of us find activities that require more complex skills, including cognitive ones, more satisfying. That's why people who know how to play bridge generally prefer it to Go Fish.

The more complex forms of cooperation that new cognitive enhancements make possible are likely to be more intrinsically rewarding. They might make the most sophisticated forms of cooperation to date look like Go Fish.

Some anti-enhancement writers, including Michael Sandel, think that those who take a more favorable view of enhancements fail to see that social practices have their own internal goods. They worry that enhancements will disrupt existing social practices and deprive us of the goods that are internal to them. That's a legitimate worry. Some enhancements may disrupt some valuable social practices and some may not. But what these writers overlook is the fact that the kind of social practices we have, and therefore the kinds of goods available to us, depend upon our capacities. If we choose wisely in improving our capacities, we will no doubt develop new social practices, and these will include new goods. This has happened before. The historical enhancements—literacy, numeracy, institutions, and science—have led to the development of more complex social practices that have provided new goods, new sources of flourishing.

The instrumental benefits of widespread biomedical cognitive enhancements are likely to be similar to those we've already gotten from literacy, numeracy, computers, and science: We'd be better able to solve social, medical, and environmental problems, so far as the solutions depend on knowledge and cooperation. But the intrinsic benefits shouldn't be underestimated. Think about how impoverished your mental and emotional life would be if you couldn't read. Your knowledge of the natural world and of human life would be pitifully scant, and the scope of your sympathy and empathy would be cramped. Although it is hard for us to imagine, our biomedically enhanced descendants may think that the life of individuals whose cognitive enhancements were limited to the nonbiomedical variety would be equally impoverished.

Why Governments Will Care About Enhancements

So far I've explained why it's a mistake to think that biomedical enhancements will be mere personal goods or zero-sum affairs. That takes care of two of the key false framing assumptions that have distorted the debate about enhancement. The key feature of enhancements that makes them social rather than merely personal goods, and that creates opportunities for win-win situations is their contribution to productivity. Governments typically care a lot about productivity. In our world, failed states aside, people expect their governments to create the conditions for economic prosperity. We also tend to think that economic prosperity means economic growth.

The Harvard economist Benjamin Friedman has a fascinating view about why economic growth is *morally* imperative. He cites evidence that people tend to think their lives are going well only if one or the other of two conditions holds: They think they are doing better than those around them or they think they will be better off in the future than they are now. Friedman concludes, quite reasonably, that we'd all be better off if people's sense of well-being didn't depend on their thinking they are doing better than those around them. (It's only in Lake Wobegon that all the children can be above average.) If we have to depend on thinking that we're doing better than those around us for our sense of well-being, we will be in a zero-sum situation: Life *will* be like a fiercely competitive game. So, it's much better if we believe that we'll do better in the future than we're doing now. For that belief to be stable, it has to be well founded, and it will only be well founded if there is economic growth. So, in Friedman's view, we need economic growth, not because it's good in itself, but because a society in which there's economic growth will tend to be morally better. Economic growth will allow better relationships among people, avoiding destructive envy.

Friedman's moral case for economic growth is intriguing. It's plausible enough to add considerable weight to the standard case for growth, namely, that it is generally a precondition for people being able to better their condition. The combined weight of these two arguments for growth transfers to the case for biomedical enhancements, so far as they increase productivity.

Governments want their citizens to feel optimistic about the future. If they don't feel that way, they're likely to blame the government. They also want their citizens to be productive, for their own reasons. A more productive country is more powerful and governments tend to crave power above all else. Consider the rationale for the modern "welfare state" that emerged in Europe in the late nineteenth century. For the first time, the state defined its role to include the provision of basic education, health insurance, and unemployment insurance. Typically the justification given for this massive change included an appeal to productivity and economic growth. A strong nation required a strong economy, and a strong economy requires healthy, educated citizens.

Most participants in the debate about biomedical enhancements assume that they will be market goods. Making that assumption produces a certain picture of the moral issues. If you think that biomedical enhancements will be market goods, created by private companies in pursuit of profit, and available to individuals according to their preferences and ability to pay, you'll draw two conclusions. First, you'll assume that *the* big ethical issue is distributive justice: If biomedical enhancements are as valuable as we think they are going to be, isn't it wrong for them to be distributed according to ability to pay? Wouldn't that be just as wrong, or almost as wrong, as allowing basic medical care to be available only to those who can pay for it? Second, you'll assume that the only role for the government will be to regulate the market in enhancements—to make sure they are safe and effective.

The picture changes dramatically once we see that some biomedical enhancements will be very attractive to governments. They'll care greatly about the development and wide diffusion of those enhancements that promise to increase productivity. They'll also be interested in those that reduce social costs—or rather, government costs. For example, there's solid evidence that people who are at the low end of the normal distribution of intelligence tend to have a lot more problems—alcoholism and drug abuse, domestic violence, mental illness, physical illness, and collisions with the law. The modern state has to deal with these problems and doing so is expensive. Suppose governments think that boosting intelligence for these big-ticket citizens—or enhancing their "good" motivation—would reduce these costs. Whether they are right or wrong about this, governments are likely to be sympathetic to proposals to undertake this sort of enhancement. They may subsidize its development and its use, and they may strongly "encourage" people to avail themselves of it.

This point about reducing social costs may provoke a bout of déjà vu in some readers: Didn't those nasty old eugenicists think that government-driven compulsory sterilizations were needed to reduce social costs that the genetically disadvantaged imposed on the rest of us? Yes, that's true, but notice that in saying that people with low intelligence have more problems (with correspondingly higher costs, if society tries to cope with them), we needn't and shouldn't assume, as the eugenicists did, that low intelligence is "genetically determined." And notice also that biomedical enhancement, unlike eugenic sterilization, needn't aim to prevent high-cost individuals from being born. Instead, nongenetic enhancements would be aimed at reducing the suffering of existing individuals.

Most bioethicists I know don't even consider the possibility that the government may take an interest in biomedical enhancements. Perhaps this is because they tend to think of biomedical enhancements as personal goods. There may be another reason: They assume that the bitter aftertaste of the eugenics movement has taught us a lesson: At least in liberal, constitutional democracies with entrenched individual rights, we'll be smart enough not to allow government to fiddle with our biology ever again.

That's naïve overconfidence at its worst. To justify encouraging or even requiring biomedical enhancements, governments wouldn't have to resurrect the bad science and bizarre master-race theories that warped eugenic thinking. They would only have to appeal to the same reasons we all invoke when we justify public education, health insurance, public health measures like vaccination, and policies designed to help American business be more competitive in a globalized economy. So, the bad news is that we can't say, "We've learned our lesson from eugenics; at least we don't have to worry about government-directed enhancement; we can concentrate on the ethical problems of laissez-faire enhancement." We need to prepare ourselves for the risk of the wrong sort of government involvement in the development and diffusion of biomedical enhancements.

The good news is that if governments do become involved, this may ease the distributive justice problem. If some enhancements are treated like public education or basic health care, then governments will try to ensure that they are widely distributed. That means that who gets them won't be simply a matter of who can pay. Government involvement won't eliminate inequalities in the distribution of these enhancements, but it will limit their magnitude.

There's one last assumption that has distorted the framing of the justice or fairness issues. It's widely assumed that biomedical enhancements will be so expensive that many people won't be able to afford them. That's a very broad and wholly unfounded generalization. It's also a generalization that doesn't take time into account.

Once again, we have to avoid biomedical enhancement exceptionalism. We need to think of biomedical enhancements as one kind of innovation among others. Some very valuable innovations become inexpensive pretty quickly. Here are two examples among many: cell phones and prescription medicines, once they go off patent and can be produced as generics.

No doubt some people thought, not so long ago, that cell phones would be expensive toys for the rich. They were profoundly mistaken. The number of cell phones in use worldwide has skyrocketed, with some countries, including Nigeria and Russia, showing an increase in cell phone ownership of as much as 57% between 2002 and 2007. As I mentioned earlier, some of the world's poorest people now have cell phones, and this communication enhancement has been remarkably empowering. People are using cell phones in many ways, from boosting their economic productivity to holding governments accountable. Computers have followed the same trajectory, though perhaps not as quickly as cell phones: They've become much more powerful and empowering, and much cheaper.

Recently a team of scientists at MIT announced an inexpensive add-on technology for cell phones that sounds almost too good to be true. It's a kind of computerized microscope cum laboratory. The MIT team says it can be added during the production of standard cell phones at a cost of around $1.00. The new device allows instant analysis of water, blood, and other liquids and can transmit the results wirelessly to environmental agencies, public health agencies, or other groups. There's a crucial, very general lesson here: How expensive an enhancement is will depend on whether it can be cheaply piggybacked on enhancements or other innovations that are already widely used.

Perhaps people wrongly assume that biomedical enhancements will be expensive because they overgeneralize from an unrepresentative sample. If you focus on genetic engineering of embryos or fancy brain/computer technologies, you'll think big bucks. You'll also think that enhancement won't be available in poor countries because they lack the infrastructure to support such technologies. But there are two reasons not to think in this way. First, even those exotic technologies may become cheap eventually and perhaps rather rapidly. Second, for the foreseeable future, the most important biomedical enhancements are likely to be drugs. Drugs require considerably less in the way of infrastructure than fancier biomedical interventions. Drugs that are like vaccines—ones that don't have to be administered daily—require less infrastructure than those that do. Drugs also become very cheap once they go off patent. Walmart offers dozens of prescription drugs in generic form at $4.00 for a thirty-day supply. That's thirty times cheaper than a month of daily lattes at Starbucks. Someday Walmart's list may include cognitive enhancement drugs that are a lot more effective than caffeine.

Under existing intellectual property laws, when a company gets a patent for a new drug, it gets a monopoly on the production of the drug for the patent period, usually twenty years. This means that the patent holder has the exclusive right to produce the drug during that period. It also has the right to sell licenses to others to produce the drug. If anybody else produces the drug without a license, they infringe the patent and are subject to legal liability. Having a patent allows a company to engage in "monopoly pricing"—*it* sets the price, not the interaction of supply and demand as in a competitive market. The justification for having patents and thus for allowing monopoly pricing is to give would-be innovators an incentive to expend the resources and bear the risks of the research enterprise.

How soon drugs go off patent and become radically cheaper is a function of the patent period under existing intellectual property laws. Intellectual property laws aren't like laws of nature; we made them and in principle we can change them. Any viable set of intellectual property laws will have to give sufficient incentives for innovation, but there's no reason to believe that existing intellectual property laws are optimal. If we value justice as well as innovation, we may need to strike a different balance, by shortening the patent period or tweaking the system in some other way.

The effects of monopoly pricing are especially troubling in the case of "essential medicines"—medicines to treat HIV-AIDS and other drugs that disproportionately affect the world's poorest people. If the prices of such drugs are too high, tens of millions of people will die because they can't afford them.

There are a number of proposals on the table for modifying existing intellectual property laws to make "essential medicines" more affordable. An international relations scholar, an international lawyer, and I have recently proposed a more general modification of intellectual property laws. This relatively minor modification would address not only the problem of essential medicines, but also a more general problem: When a valuable innovation is not becoming widely available fast enough, how can we speed up its diffusion? The problem of inadequate diffusion of valuable biomedical technologies fits under this general heading.

In a nutshell, our proposal is for a new international institution that would have three main functions. First, it would set up a prize fund for rewarding "diffusion entrepreneurship"—providing prestigious cash rewards to individuals or groups who devise ways of speeding up the diffusion of valuable innovations, as with piggybacking. Second, it would monitor valuable innovations, including biomedical enhancements, to determine whether they are diffusing rapidly enough to avoid serious injustices. More specifically, it would determine whether the monopoly prices that current intellectual property rules allow are getting in the way of wider diffusion, when inadequate diffusion either contributes to severe deprivation or promotes domination and exploitation. Third, if the institution determines that this is happening, then it would issue a warning to the patent holders: Lower your prices or we'll step in and issue licenses to others to produce your product, free of charge, to lower prices and speed up diffusion in those areas where it's not diffusing rapidly enough. The idea is that the threat of issuing licenses would give the producers of innovations an incentive to reduce their prices. Of course, if the threat became a reality, the producers would have to be compensated—that's only fair. But the idea is that the amount of compensation would be lower than what the producers could get if they were allowed to continue to exercise their monopoly-pricing privilege. If the system were working well, the threat would rarely if ever be carried out. The credibility of the threat would mitigate the problem of injustice in the diffusion of innovations.

Our proposal includes a lot more details, including the way it fits with existing international law. I've only sketched it here in barest outlines to make a general point: There are ways of modifying existing intellectual property laws to help reduce the risk that innovations—including biomedical enhancements—will worsen existing injustices.

The bigger point is that it's simply a mistake to assume that biomedical enhancements will be expensive. They may or may not be expensive at first, but how long they remain expensive is up to us. We can make them cheaper either by modifying intellectual property laws or by having government subsidize them. If governments view some enhancements as on a par with public education, they will presumably subsidize them.

There's a catch: If governments think certain enhancements are valuable enough to subsidize, they may also want to make them mandatory. That would be especially troubling for some enhancements, especially those that involved genetic changes. It might be somewhat less troubling for cognitive enhancement drugs.

Nevertheless, the prospect of government mandating any biomedical enhancement is problematic. People who object to mandatory vaccinations or even mandatory schooling will no doubt be even more disturbed by the prospect of mandatory biomedical enhancements (though it's not clear why they should be). Fortunately, government subsidies aren't the only way to reduce the risk that biomedical enhancements will worsen injustices. Modifying intellectual property laws to reduce costs and thereby speed diffusion is probably a much safer alternative.

Willing Guinea Pigs

It's true that many innovations are at first available only to the rich. Whether this inequality is unjust is a complicated matter, as we've seen. A lot depends on whether privileged access to an innovation puts the lucky few in a position to exploit or dominate others. That's less likely if the innovation becomes more widely available pretty quickly. But there's another variable here worth considering: risk. Think of wealthy people who like new stuff as *volunteer risk-pioneers*. They perform a valuable service: They buy the first-generation version of the innovation at a high price. Often, they get a defective product and sometimes a dangerous one. Later, when the bugs have been eliminated and the safety issues have been dealt with, you and I buy the improved version at a lower price. How's that for a deal? And we don't even have to force them to do it.

If you're worried about biomedical enhancements having unintended bad consequences, you should be especially grateful that there are volunteer risk-pioneers. They'll be the guinea pigs and if the experiment goes awry, the damage will be limited to them. If you're worried about unfairness, the volunteer risk-pioneer phenomenon should provide some consolation: The rich get benefits before the rest of us, but they also bear greater risks and costs.

The Positive Side: Inequality-Reducing Innovations

So far we've concentrated only on the risk that biomedical enhancements will worsen unjust inequalities. It's equally important to remember that many technological innovations lessen unjust inequalities. We already encountered a striking, very recent example: the Ushahidi Web platform, which increases government accountability, in effect shifting the balance of power a bit toward the citizens and away from the government. Cell phones with cameras are another example: Increasingly, people use them to record police brutality and this does something to reduce the dangerous power asymmetry between citizens and the police. Here are a few other examples.

- Inexpensive calculators level the playing field for the mathematically challenged.
- Medical innovations can remove or ameliorate disabilities and the inequalities they spawn.
- Internet access to medical information reduces the asymmetry of knowledge between physicians and patients, and enables patients to avoid being in an utterly dependent, subordinate position vis-à-vis their physicians.
- Affordable computers allow small businesses to reduce their marketing costs, identify low-cost inputs for their products, manage distribution, and thereby compete more effectively with big, established companies.

In all of these cases, innovations reduce morally problematic inequalities. We don't know whether biomedical enhancements will tend to exacerbate existing unjust inequalities or reduce them, overall. There is some encouraging evidence in the case of cognitive enhancement drugs: The ones that are now being used (the backdoor spin-offs from treatment drugs) seem to give the biggest boost to those who are at the low end of the normal distribution of the cognitive skills they affect. In that sense, they lessen inequalities rather than widening them. (The same appears to be true of SAT and LSAT prep courses.) We don't know whether that will be typical of other types of cognitive enhancements or of new cognitive enhancement drugs. Clearly, one of the crucial questions to ask when making decisions about whether social resources should be invested in the development of a biomedical enhancement is whether it is likely to worsen or reduce existing unjust inequalities.

The argument of this chapter has had some surprising twists and turns. I won't attempt a comprehensive summary. The main results are these. (1) Biomedical enhancements, like any other beneficial innovations, including the great nonbiomedical enhancements we've already achieved, carry a risk that they will worsen existing injustices, at least in the short run. (2) If the risk has been worth taking with all the other developments that have enriched our lives, it's hard to see that it would be any different with biomedical enhancements—at least those that are likely to yield significant social benefits. (3) The right thing to do is to try to make sure that the really valuable biomedical enhancements don't remain the exclusive possession of the rich long enough to cause trouble. To do that, we'll need to learn all we can about how valuable innovations have diffused in the past and then use that knowledge to speed up the diffusion of the best biomedical enhancements. (4) We should be deeply concerned about the risk that biomedical enhancements will worsen unjust inequalities; but we shouldn't lose sight of the fact that they may also present new possibilities for making society more just. (5) Although the risk of injustice is great and will require imaginative institutional innovations, there is no reason at present to think that we should take the radical (and impractical) step of trying to ban biomedical enhancements in the name of justice.

6 | IS ENHANCEMENT CORRUPTING?

Stirring, Yes; But What Does It Mean?

Professor Michael Sandel of Harvard University fears we're on the brink of a dire shortage—a shortage of *lack* of control over our lives. He says that embracing biomedical enhancements "threatens" to produce a situation in which there will be "nothing to contemplate outside our own wills." If that stirring phrase means anything, it means that biomedical enhancement could eventually eliminate chance. In other words, if we pursue biomedical enhancements far enough, they will eventually give us *total control*. Sandel thinks that human life would be impoverished if this occurred. He likes the fact that we lack control, partly because it instills the virtue of humility.

The prediction that biomedical enhancement could lead to total control is an odd one to make, unless you're an ultra-extreme genetic determinist. Suppose—and this now more science fantasy than fiction—that prospective parents could pick and choose from a large array of genes and select the ones they prefer their child to have. That wouldn't eliminate chance from human life! There would be a lot to contemplate other than "our own will."

For one thing, there would still be random mutations of genes. But that's only a tiny part of the story. There would still be vast areas

of lack of control in human life in general, including our relationships with our children. Regardless of how they get their genes, once
children develop enough, they make choices—and some of their
choices conflict with what their parents want for them.

Even with thoroughgoing biomedical enhancement, our lives
would still be subject to a massive lack of control. Wars would still
occur; unpredicted and unwanted economic upheavals would still
happen; natural disasters would still erupt. Pandemics would break
out as pathogens mutate into strains we lack resistance to. Individuals
would still train for jobs that disappear; entrepreneurs would lose
everything despite having made perfectly reasonable predictions
about what the market will be like; people would still fall in love at
the most improbable moments with the most improbable people.
The interactions of individuals would still lead to unpredictable and
uncontrollable consequences.

Only a genetic determinist on steroids (so to speak) could think
that there would be "nothing left to contemplate but our own wills"
even if we were able to go a lot farther down the road to biomedical
enhancements than we are ever likely to go. Mastery of human
biology wouldn't be mastery of the human condition. And mastery
of our children's biology wouldn't be mastery of their lives. There's no
risk of a lack of control shortage. So there's no risk of a lack of opportunities for exhibiting the virtue of humility. Sandel's claim that we
face a threat of total control, taken at face value, is patently absurd.

This applies to the good as well as the bad in our lives. Even in a
world of pervasive and powerful biomedical enhancements, we'd
still have plenty of opportunities for appreciating that many of the
good things in our lives are not our accomplishments, not subject to
our wills. We'd still be in a position to show gratitude for many
"gifts"—to feel fortunate that we met the right person at the right
time, that we happened to choose a career that turned out to be

economically rewarding, that we happened to be born in a country with decent government and a thriving economy, that our daughters were born into a society that has begun to treat women as equals, etc., etc.

Perhaps Sandel's anti-enhancement fervor has caused rhetorical excess. Perhaps his main point can be stated without making the absurd prediction that enhancement could or will banish chance in human affairs. He thinks that what's really wrong with biomedical enhancements is not that they might have unintended bad *effects*, like destroying human nature (or creating a shortage of lack of control). For him, the big problem is that *the very pursuit of enhancements*—quite apart from its effects—is a sign of bad character.

The bad character is of two main sorts, according to Sandel. First, he thinks that to want to enhance ourselves is to desire not just improvement but perfection. That's why his book condemning biomedical enhancement bears the title *The Case Against Perfection*. Sandel thinks that the desire for perfection is a vice—that people who desire perfection, in themselves or their children, have a character defect. Notice: He thinks *all* striving for perfection is a vice. He doesn't consider the fact that he's apparently committed to the view that religiously motivated striving for perfection is a vice. But let that pass.

Second, he thinks that to pursue enhancements is a sure sign that we have another vice: unwillingness to leave ourselves "open to the unbidden." Or as he also puts it, pursuing enhancements betrays a failure to appreciate the "giftedness" of life—the fact that much of what is valuable in our lives is not the result of our own action and hence isn't something we can take credit for.

For Sandel, being open to the unbidden involves more than simply not seeking total mastery or perfection; it also means accepting what chance delivers. Sandel thinks that parents who try to use biomedical enhancements to shape the characteristics of their children lack the virtue of openness to the unbidden. He thinks that being a good parent means accepting your child's imperfections. Let's consider each of these two claims about character—the one about the craving for perfection and the one about openness to the unbidden.

The claim that the pursuit of biomedical enhancement is the pursuit of perfection is a sweeping, wildly implausible generalization about human motivation—and an extremely uncharitable one. Why on earth would anyone think that whenever we want to improve some capacity, we are pursuing perfection? To pursue enhancement is to strive for *improvement* of some capacity or trait. Improvement is not perfection. It might be true that *some* people who want enhancements have an *unlimited* desire for improvement—that they want to become perfect—but there's no reason to think that everybody or even most people are that way. What evidence is there that people who opt for better than 20/20 correction with laser surgery or people like Michelle who take Ritalin to concentrate better are pursuing perfection rather than improvement? Absolutely none. Sandel doesn't seem to think he needs evidence. He just makes pronouncements.

Sandel repeatedly emphasizes that what's really wrong, or most seriously wrong with enhancement is not its effects: "I do not think that the main problem with enhancement and genetic engineering is that they undermine effort and erode human agency. The deeper danger is that they represent a kind of hyper-agency, a Promethean aspiration to remake nature, including our own human nature, to serve our purposes and satisfy our desires. The problem is . . . the drive to mastery."

Think about that for a moment. Is it true that whenever someone tries to enhance a human capacity they're doing so "represents" the drive to mastery? I'm not sure what "represents" is supposed to mean here. Sandel never explains it. He may mean that the attempt to enhance is *caused* by the drive to master or that it is an *expression of* the "drive to mastery." As we've already seen, if "the drive to mastery" means striving for perfection or total control, then in either case what he's saying is clearly false. Trying to enhance some human capacity doesn't mean you are trying to achieve perfection or total control. There are many reasons for undertaking particular enhancements other than the pursuit of perfection or total control, and people can have a number of different motivations for seeking to enhance. It's just a cheap rhetorical trick to say or even to suggest that whenever people try to enhance human capacities they are "really" striving for mastery or perfection.

Remember: Sandel can't reply that he means that employing biomedical enhancements will cause us to desire perfection or total control. He says over and over that the problem with enhancement is not its *effects*, but what it "*represents*."

Does Sandel think that it is only biomedical enhancements that "represent" the drive to mastery? He doesn't say so. In fact, just the opposite: He seems to think that there's something wrong with enhancement per se, no matter what means we employ to achieve it. So it looks like he is committed also to the bizarre claim that whenever you try to enhance your child's cognition by teaching him to read, what you are doing "represents" the drive to mastery. Any attempt to enhance—or to have any effect at all in the world—is an effort to exert *some* control, but that's hardly objectionable. Mastery presumably means total control. To call the effort to exert *some* control the "drive to mastery" is exaggeration bordering on the hysterical.

In some cases, a particular attempt to enhance *might* be the result of someone's (delusional) striving for perfection or mastery, but that doesn't mean that enhancement—all or most cases of it—are wrong.

Sandel says he's trying to ascertain "the moral status of enhancement" itself, not its effects. Particular attempts to enhance can have a moral status—they can be good or bad or indifferent, depending on the context, the agent's motivations, the consequences, etc. But enhancement as such doesn't have a moral status. Trying to ascertain the moral status of enhancement makes about as much sense as trying to ascertain the moral status of human action. Sandel thinks that enhancement has the moral status of being impermissible, but that's because he wrongly thinks that enhancement as such is an instance of or "represents" the "drive to mastery."

When he's railing against genetic enhancement of children, Sandel refers to "hyperparenting." He has in mind parents who try too hard to make their kids smarter or more athletic using conventional means like tutoring or tennis camp. They're control freaks, and they place unconscionable demands on their children. Of course, some parents do go too far in trying to help their children develop. But it's a huge leap from that fact to the conclusion that the pursuit of biomedical enhancements or even genetic enhancements is a quest for perfection, whenever it occurs, or even usually. We've seen this kind of motivational smear campaign before: In chapter 3 I noted that Bush's Council (of which Sandel was a member) insinuated that virtually anybody who wants to reproduce by cloning has disgusting motives (they're trying to recreate dead children; they think they are so great that the world needs more "copies" of them; or they're trying to design their children according to their own tastes, etc.). Similarly, Sandel may think he can discredit enhancement through guilt by association with "hyperparenting."

He also writes as if it's obvious that people who want to enhance their children's capacities are only trying to improve their competitive edge, to enable them to win out in competitions with others. That's a pretty sweeping and unflattering claim about the motivation of parents who seek enhancements for their children. Leon Kass is doing the same sort of thing when he says that people who say they want to extend human life really crave immortality. Impugning peoples' motives instead of giving reasons why their views are false is no way to get at the truth.

Sandel and Bush's Council don't begin to provide evidence to support the sweeping claims they make about the motivation of those they disagree with. Different people will have different motives for pursuing biomedical enhancements, and many will have mixed motives. The same is true for parents who send their children to Harvard. It would be just as crazy to say that everybody who sends their child to Harvard is only, or primarily, concerned with giving them a competitive edge, as it would be to say that anybody who employs biomedical enhancements is similarly motivated. Sandel's insinuation that parents who use biomedical means to enhance their children's capacities are striving to make them better competitors is another unsupported, uncharitable generalization. When you try to help your child be a better reader or thinker, this doesn't mean you are striving to help him beat other children in some sort of competition. So why must the desire to use *biomedical* enhancements betray an obsession with competitiveness?

Freud, referring to the then-prevalent preoccupation with his idea of phallic symbols, once famously said: "Sometimes a cigar is just a cigar." Likewise, sometimes—I imagine quite often—an enhancement is just an enhancement, not the pursuit of perfection. You *might* be seeking an enhancement as a step toward the goal of perfection, but you won't be doing this unless you are deluded about the power of biomedical technologies. If you are reasonably well informed and not subject to delusions of grandeur, you'll pursue an enhancement for one or the other of two reasons, neither of which has anything to do with a desire for perfection or mastery. First, you may believe, quite reasonably, that improving a particular capacity will make you better off overall or that if lots of people have this improvement we'll all benefit. Second, you may believe, again quite reasonably, that improving some capacity is necessary to avoid a worsening of our situation (remember Tancredi's point).

Maybe Sandel's point isn't that seeking biomedical enhancements is always or even usually a quest for perfection (or a sign of ruthless competitiveness). Maybe it's that in a world where there are lots of opportunities for biomedical enhancement, there's a *risk* that we'll get carried away and overdo it. If that's what he means, then he's right. That's an important message, but it's not nearly as exciting (or original) as it seemed when it was swathed in over-heated rhetoric.

It's one thing to say that there's a risk that we'll overdo it, but quite another to say that this risk is so grave that we're better off abstaining from biomedical enhancements across the board. Almost everything involves risks. Sandel seems to assume that the risk of indulging the vices of perfectionism and "closedness" to the unbidden is so grave in the case of biomedical enhancements that we should just say no. He ignores the fact that if the benefits of doing something are great enough, then some risks may be acceptable.

Sandel says that the ethics of enhancement isn't merely a matter of costs and benefits. That's true if being a matter of costs and benefits means that we can mechanically calculate the right answer after neatly quantifying the pros and cons. We can't do that, of course. But we can and should recognize that in thinking about whether to enhance we have to look at the positives as well as the negatives. And of course in doing so we should be aware that the possible negatives include the risk that pursuing enhancements can *sometimes* manifest bad character or contribute to it. Fair enough, but that's not an "argument against enhancement." Not by a long shot.

Remember how extreme Sandel's formulation of the risk is: He thinks that people who use biomedical enhancements are striving for total control. Or, on a less extreme interpretation, he thinks that pursuing enhancements poses a very serious risk that we will strive for total control. But as I've already noted, anybody who thinks that biomedical enhancements can give us total control over human existence is deluded to the point of madness. So Sandel seems to be committed to the view that the risk of people insanely overestimating the power of biomedical enhancements is so serious that we should forgo all of the benefits that biomedical enhancements could bring! Rather than forgoing the benefits of biomedical enhancements, wouldn't it be better to provide treatment for those people who are so deluded as to think that total mastery is possible? Of course, we don't know if there are many people like that. Sandel assumes that the delusional drive for mastery is a mammoth problem—so big that it requires forgoing all enhancements—but he doesn't provide any evidence that it is. Anecdotal reference to "hyperparenting" is not adequate evidence for the claim that there is any such massive delusion.

What would account for the conspicuous absence in Sandel's thinking of any attempt to weigh the negatives of enhancement against the positives? Perhaps he has a skewed understanding of what the positives are. Sandel tends to write as if the benefits of biomedical enhancements are vanity goods or zero-sum goods. Maybe that makes sense, if your paradigm is "hyperparenting" or cosmetic surgery, but it's very misleading when you consider the full range of benefits that various biomedical enhancements could bring. As I argued in earlier chapters, some biomedical enhancements will be positive-sum and they'll bring very significant benefits, for us as individuals and for society.

What about the virtue of openness to the unbidden (or, as he also calls it, appreciation of "giftedness")? Sandel stakes a lot on this supposed virtue but says remarkably little about it. His attack on enhancement is supposed to be based on the importance of this virtue, but he never says what it is to have it. He's what moral philosophers call a virtue theorist, but without a theory of virtue. Of course, it's true that in *some sense* parents should accept their children's imperfections, but the question is *in what sense*? After all, sometimes parents should accept their children's imperfections, but sometimes they shouldn't. If I have a child with cleft palate, I'm a callous jerk if I say to the surgeon who wants to repair it: "No thanks: I've got unconditional love for my child; his cleft palate was unbidden. I'm remaining open to it. I appreciate the giftedness of life."

What we need is a convincing account of when we ought to accept problems and when we should try to solve them. Sandel doesn't provide it. He thinks it's all right to treat or prevent disease but never all right to enhance. In other words, he says that we should only intervene to restore our "natural functioning." He fails to see that the natural isn't always good or even acceptable. I suspect that he's stuck in the pre-Darwinian, teleological view of nature that I criticized in earlier chapters.

Sandel tries to shore up his view that we should only treat or prevent disease and not enhance by saying that the good of medicine is health, not enhancement. He says that if you understand medicine as a social practice, you'll understand that its good (or aim) is health, not enhancement. That may be true, but it tells us *nothing* about whether we should use biomedical enhancements. There's an obvious reason why the social practice we call medicine has been limited to the pursuit of health, that is, the curing or prevention of disease: until recently that's the most we were capable of.

The question we now face is whether we should develop new social practices that go beyond the treatment and prevention of disease to encompass biomedical enhancement. Don't be confused by the occurrence of "medical" in "biomedical enhancements." Put the question this way: Should we use *biotechnologies* to enhance human capacities? No amount of reflection on the nature of medicine as a social practice can answer that question. (Notice: It isn't part of the meaning of "biotechnologies" that they are only properly used to further the aims of medicine.)

Let's pursue this idea that it's wrong for parents to use biotechnologies for the purpose of enhancement. Often the right thing to do is to try to improve your child's "natural gifts," even when this isn't a matter of correcting a defect, a failure of natural functioning. That's what education is about. It's ironic that Sandel teaches at Harvard, lecturing to many students who are there because their parents wanted to give them the best cognitive enhancement money can buy. Sandel never succeeds in explaining why traditional, non-biomedical enhancements of our children or ourselves are all right, but those involving biotechnologies are either sure signs of vice or pose an unacceptable risk of it. That's an impossible task: You can't get from the true but almost vacuous claim that we shouldn't overdo the quest for improvement to the conclusion that biomedical enhancements, or even genetic enhancements, are always or even usually vicious.

You may think I've been pretty hard on Sandel. Don't get me wrong. I think he is right to emphasize that we need to consider our motives for seeking enhancement. I also think he's right to be concerned that we may get carried away with enhancement. In fact, I'm so impressed with these points that I'm now going to try to develop them carefully, without misleading, hysterical rhetoric.

Concerns Aren't Arguments

Before we go any further, I want to emphasize a simple, but absolutely crucial distinction. It's one thing to raise a *concern* about enhancement—a "con" or cost broadly considered. It's quite another to show that the concern is so serious that it constitutes an *argument* against enhancement. An argument against enhancement is a piece of reasoning that ends with the conclusion: "It's wrong to enhance." We have concerns about lots of things that aren't wrong to do, all things considered. For example, we have concerns about democracy. Democratic political processes can lead to mistakes. Sometimes democracy underutilizes good information, because popular but uninformed people get elected. Sometimes the majority makes other mistakes. But that isn't an "argument against democracy"—it's only a concern. To use slightly different language, democracy has costs, but we think the benefits outweigh the costs. Or, if "costs" and "benefits" sound too quantitative and mechanical, let's say that we think there are cons as well as pros when it comes to democracy, but that on balance the pros outweigh the cons. Merely pointing out a concern about enhancement isn't the same as showing that there's an objection—a *conclusive* consideration—against it. The odd thing about people like Sandel and the other members of Bush's Council who raise character concerns about enhancement is that they act as if these concerns were anti-enhancement arguments. They don't take seriously the possibility that the considerations in favor of enhancement may outweigh the concerns. They just point out a risk and then conclude that enhancement is wrong.

There's one other point to keep in mind before we try to make better sense of the character concerns that Sandel raises than he does. Remember that he thinks that the pursuit of biomedical enhancements, or at least genetic enhancements, betrays an unseemly craving for mastery and a failure to be open to the unbidden. But why, if this is the case, does it only apply to those sorts of enhancements, rather than enhancements across the board—literacy, numeracy, the agrarian revolution, cell phones, computers, and institutions? All of these nonbiomedical enhancements carry a risk that the pursuit of improvement will become a quest for perfection (for some people, anyway). And all of them imply a refusal to accept things as they are, an effort to exert greater control over our lives. The big problem is that Sandel never succeeds in showing why biomedical enhancements, or those biomedical enhancements that involve genetic engineering, are so different from the great historical enhancements that he can consistently condemn the former without (absurdly) condemning the latter. So, as we try to make sense of character concerns about biomedical enhancement, we'll need to think about the implications for other enhancements. That will serve as a reality check: It will help us avoid the mistake of thinking that concerns about biomedical enhancement are always conclusive objections.

Appreciating What We Have

There's an advantage to thinking about appreciation for what we have rather than about "giftedness": It doesn't assume that what we have is a gift from God. In this book, I'm avoiding religious assumptions. That's not because I'm antireligious. I'm simply trying to discuss enhancement in ways that are accessible to most people, whether they are religious or not. So let's stick with the idea that appreciation for what we have is a virtue, a good character trait. I think we can agree that it is and then see what the implications for enhancement are.

Why is appreciation for what we have a virtue? To answer that question, we need to say a little about what virtues are. They're character traits. In fact, they're pretty complicated character traits. They involve having certain feelings, making certain kinds of evaluations, and acting in certain ways. Traditionally, virtues are also thought to be character traits that are generally valuable to have and that generally make those that have them valuable to other people as well.

That's all very well and good, but too general. What's valuable about having the character trait of appreciating what we have? Why should we be appreciative? The first thing to notice is that, properly described, the virtue in question is *proper* appreciation of what we have. You can go wrong in appreciating something, in either of two directions. You can value it too much or too little. The parent who doesn't accept the surgeon's offer to repair her child's cleft palate goes too far in appreciating "the given." How might we go too far in the other direction? What counts as underappreciation? Or, to put it in slightly different terms: What are some of the ways our attitudes toward what we have can show character flaws? I can think of several ways.

First, if you constantly focus on future goods—things you don't have now but would like to have—you won't fully *enjoy* the good things you already have. In many cases, the benefit we get from what we have achieved is lessened if we don't focus on it. Here's an example. Suppose I work hard to buy a beautiful home because I think that I'll really enjoy living in it. But then I decide that I also want an expensive car. In order to afford both the home and the expensive car, I have to work longer hours. That means I'm not at home as much and so I don't get as much enjoyment from my home as I could. Or, suppose I've got enough time to enjoy my home, but I'm constantly distracted by thoughts of new acquisitions. Again, the result is that I don't enjoy my home as I ought to. I think we all know people who set one "consumption goal" after another—they work harder to buy more and more stuff—but they don't seem to get much enjoyment out of what they have. It all seems rather futile, self-frustrating.

The highly original economist Robert Frank has written an intriguing book called *Luxury Fever*. There's a rather harsh joke about economists: They're good with figures but lack the personality to be accountants. That's not true of lots of economists, but especially not true of Frank. With wit and grace, he shows how the pursuit of ever-higher quality consumer goods can make us worse off, not better off. In our terminology, Frank shows that an endless quest for *enhanced* consumer goods—cars, computers, sound systems, kitchen appliances, etc.—is self-defeating, even self-destructive. The problem is really twofold. First, as we've already seen, if you're constantly focused on the next higher-quality item, you won't get much enjoyment out of what you already have. Second, if you're always pursuing ever-higher-quality items you're overlooking the fact that to get them you have to bear costs—you have to give up something valuable (money, leisure time, etc.)—and that in many cases you're better off *overall* if you settle for something that is *good enough*, even though it's not the best.

A person who constantly pursued improvements, either in ordinary consumer goods or in his own traits, would be foolish, because he would be on an acquisition treadmill. He would lack the virtue of prudence or proper self-regard. He would also suffer the vice of greed or insatiability: No good thing he possesses would ever be enough. A rich menu of biomedical enhancements would create new opportunities for this sort of behavior. Imagine a biomedical enhancement catalog that was a super-seductive combination of Williams-Sonoma and Victoria's Secret.

There are other ways that lack of appreciation for what we have can be a vice. If I underappreciate the goods I now have, it's not just that I will deprive myself of the full enjoyment they could bring to me. I may also be guilty of failing to appreciate their value. One way we show that we properly appreciate the value of something is by preserving it, rather than discarding it in the pursuit of something we think is better.

In some contexts, constantly striving for improvement can lead to betrayal. Imagine someone who abandons a valuable relationship whenever he has the opportunity for a better one. Such a person would be incapable of genuine commitment. Suppose your lover says to you one day: "I know we've been together a long time and you do make me very happy, but I met someone five minutes ago who I think will make me a little happier, so good-bye." If she said that, she would likely be foolish in thinking that it's possible to compare life with you, whom she's known well for a long time, with life with a person she's just met. But foolishness is not her only flaw: She also lacks the virtue of loyalty or constancy. She doesn't know what love is. Whether you should stay in a relationship does often depend upon whether your needs are being met, but that's not the same as saying that you should jump ship whenever a more attractive person happens by.

A person who "abandoned" his own self every time he saw an opportunity for improvement would also be morally defective. As the Oxford philosopher Alexandre Erler argues, being a good person means, among other things, having the right attitude toward yourself. To put it differently, part of being a healthy person is having proper self-regard and sometimes that means accepting yourself as you are. A person who relentlessly, constantly seeks to improve every trait he has shows too little self-regard; he underrates his own value. To summarize: There are a number of different ways one can go wrong by being too quick to be dissatisfied with what we have and launching off into the pursuit of something new because we think it will be better.

Treating Ourselves as Objects

There's another problem with viewing ourselves as endlessly improvable. There's the risk that we will regard ourselves as machines for producing a series of increasingly enhanced selves. I know people who act this way now, without the benefit of biomedical enhancements. In order to be slimmer, more buffed, or (if they're academics) more cultured, they drive themselves so hard that if anyone else did this to them they'd be charged with the crime of slavery. They, too, don't show proper appreciation for themselves or for the good things they already have.

In a world of biomedical enhancements, people who don't have proper appreciation for what they have will have greater opportunities for indulging their vice. But they also may have greater resources for resisting this temptation. That will depend on whether they're able to enhance their virtues or at least their ability to resist vices. Sandel and others worry that biomedical enhancements will give greater scope for vice; they don't consider the possibility that biomedical enhancements can make us morally better. More about that later.

Loss of Spontaneity

People who endlessly seek improvement live in the calculating, strategic mode: They're constantly figuring out how to bring about a better state of affairs. If their plans for improvement are ambitious enough, they crowd out everything else. They're always acting in a goal-directed way, moving stage by stage along their predetermined route to improvement. They don't have time to stop and smell the roses. Constantly striving to move forward, they don't know how to go with the flow. Because their tunnel vision is focused solely on the next goal, they miss out on a lot.

A good human life has to include calculation and striving, but it also has to leave room for allowing things to happen, for being carried along rather unreflectively by our interests and desires, in a word, for *spontaneity*. I think we especially value spontaneity in intimate personal interactions. You may recall Mr. Collins in Jane Austin's wonderful novel *Pride and Prejudice.* He's an oily, supercilious clergyman who's constantly trying to stay in the good graces of his rich patron, Lady Catherine De Bourgh. To do so, he spends hours preparing compliments to her that are designed to appear to be off the cuff but that invariably come off as laughably contrived, artificial—in a word, unspontaneous. When he proposes marriage to Ms. Bennet, instead of expressing his feelings, he launches into a formal presentation of the various reasons why he thinks he should marry. Marriage for him has nothing to do with love; it's just part of a careful long-term strategic plan. You can imagine the effect on the young lady, even if you haven't read the book or seen the film. To the extent that the relentless pursuit of enhancements would drive out spontaneity in our lives, it would be as comical—and as pathetic—as Mr. Collins's behavior.

Let's summarize the discussion so far. Depending on how weak our character is, the pursuit of enhancements could turn out to be quite risky: We may focus so much on future goods that we fail to enjoy what we have; we may treat ourselves as mere machines for producing better future selves; we may betray others for the sake of mere improvement; or we may leave no room in our lives for spontaneity.

Notice that none of these risks are unique to biomedical enhancements. We run all of these risks whenever we try to improve ourselves in any way. So *if* these risks were conclusive reasons for refraining from biomedical enhancements, they would also be conclusive reasons for refraining from *all* enhancements. But refraining from all enhancements (including literacy, numeracy, etc.) would be irrational. So, nothing we've seen so far amounts to an *argument* against biomedical enhancement. All we have—and I'm not downplaying the significance of this—is a number of risks of enhancement that we need to take into account when we weigh the pros and cons.

Before we leave the topic, let's make one more attempt to capture why appreciation for the given is important and how the availability of biomedical enhancements might diminish it. The Oxford physician-bioethicist Julian Savulescu once suggested to me that perhaps the core idea of the value of appreciation is that a good life is one in which the person concentrates on making the best of what he's been given. That reminds me of Supreme Court Justice Thurgood Marshall's statement that he hoped people would remember him as someone who "did the best he could with what he had to work with."

There's something to Savulescu's suggestion and Marshall's remark. But it's hard to know what the practical implications are. If the idea is that we should always rest content with our limitations, that's clearly wrong. Sometimes enhancing our capacity for well-being does improve our lives or prevents them from getting worse. Here's an example to show that.

Sanjay has always been athletic. His happiness depends very substantially on his ability to engage in vigorous, physically demanding sports. Sanjay worries that as he gets older, he won't be able to participate in such activities and that as a result he'll be worse off—there will be a decrease in his well-being. This worry is based on an accurate appraisal of who he is and his capacity for happiness.

Sanjay decides that it would be better, from the standpoint of his happiness, if he were to begin now to cultivate the capacity for more sedentary enjoyments—activities he'll still be able to pursue when his physical abilities diminish. He envies people who take great pleasure in long sessions of listening to music, or sitting on benches in museums contemplating great works of art, or playing bridge or chess. He'd like to be able to do that, but he quite reasonably concludes that his ability to enjoy such sedentary activities is very limited. He's tried hard to cultivate the knack, but he has failed. The music appreciation and art history courses and the bridge and chess lessons were a waste of money.

Then Sanjay learns that his efforts to cultivate the capacity for sedentary enjoyments will be more likely to succeed if he takes a particular drug. It could be a drug for attention deficit disorder, like Ritalin. Or it could be a new drug specifically designed to increase your ability to discriminate nuances in sound, while at the same time releasing the endorphins that are found in high concentrations in people who love music. If such a drug is available (and safe) Sanjay will do better if he undertakes an enhancement than if he follows the advice of making the best of what he has. He'll be better off if he enhances rather than makes the best of the hand he was dealt.

The point of this example isn't to deny that it's often good advice to make the best of what you have. Rather, it's that this generally sound counsel admits of lots of exceptions, in life generally, and perhaps especially in a world of sophisticated biomedical enhancements.

One more point about Sanjay: The enjoyment he gets from taking the drug isn't pseudo-enjoyment. It isn't passive, like the good feeling the workers get from taking soma in *Brave New World* or that heroin addicts get in our world. The drug simply enables him to engage in activities that require the exercise of skills and effort on his part. He's not taking a magic music appreciation pill; he's enhancing his ability to *develop* an appreciation for music. Here as elsewhere, biomedical determinist fantasies are to be avoided. They're not only scientifically unrealistic; they also distort our moral evaluations of enhancement.

Pseudo-Happiness

One of the most intriguing things about thinking about enhancement is that it forces you to confront some pretty basic questions—like, what is happiness, anyway? Remember, an enhancement is an improvement of some particular capacity beyond the normal. Improving a capacity doesn't necessarily make you better off, so enhancement doesn't equal a better life. (Better hearing might make you miserable if you live in a noisy environment, for example.)

The problem with the term "happiness" is that it's ambiguous. Sometimes we use it to refer to a state of pleasant contentment. But in other cases, it means something different: living well. The cases of heroin and soma addiction show that you can be happy in the first sense but not be happy in the second: living in a drug-induced state of pleasant contentment isn't living well.

Why is that? The late philosopher Robert Nozick devised a thought experiment that answers that question. Imagine that you could connect yourself to the Experience Machine. The Experience Machine can make it seem to you that you are accomplishing your most cherished goals, no matter what they are. Suppose your fondest desire is to win the Nobel Prize for Peace. The Experience Machine can stimulate your brain to produce the exact experience you would have if you won the Nobel Prize. Or suppose your fervent desire is for a famous movie star to be passionately in love with you. It can simulate what that would be like, too. It can even simulate the experience you would have if you were accepting the Nobel Prize with the movie star standing adoringly at your side.

Suppose you could be permanently connected to the Experience Machine, after you programmed in the kind of life you would like to (seem) to have and that once the machine started you wouldn't know you were connected to it. (Think of the film *The Matrix*.) You would believe that you were doing all the things it seemed you were doing. Nozick ran this thought experiment with his students at Harvard and reported that the majority said they would not take the option of having an Experience Machine "life" if it were offered.

He also thought that the majority was right. The reason most people reject the Experience Machine, Nozick surmised, is that they realize that a good human life involves more than just having certain experiences, that is, being in certain mental states. It involves really doing things, really accomplishing goals, really having meaningful relationships—not just feeling as if you did.

Nozick's thought experiment is relevant to the case of biomedical *mood* enhancement. "Mood" can mean either something that is transient or one's stable temperament—whether one has a sunny disposition or tends to have a somewhat negative outlook on life. We already have mood enhancement drugs. Drugs like Prozac (SSRIs—selective serotonin reuptake inhibitors) appear to produce some change toward the sunny side in normal people. They were first developed, not as enhancements, but to treat the disorder of depression. Here, as in other cases, enhancement came in through the back door, as an unintended result of efforts to treat a disease.

Living Authentically

Many people who don't have depression now take Prozac. This is very troubling to some people. There are two kinds of concerns. The first is that if you change your temperament by taking the drug, you won't be living *authentically*. The highly respected bioethicist David DeGrazia has argued that this needn't be the case. He notes that being authentic means living according to your own stable values. He concludes that if your desire to have a sunnier disposition is rooted in your stable values, then taking a drug to accomplish this is compatible with being authentic. In fact, many people who take Prozac describe their situation in precisely those terms: They say that taking the drug has liberated them, removed an obstacle to their being who they really are.

If you thought that all there was to a good life was having a sunny disposition, and you took Prozac to achieve this, you'd be wrong. That's the point of Nozick's thought experiment. But you wouldn't be wrong if you thought that having a sunnier disposition may make it easier for you to have a good life, by helping you to be motivated enough to accomplish what you want to accomplish, to have the relationships you value, to *live* the life you want to live.

What's the upshot of all this? It's rather simple, but important: It is one thing to take mood enhancement drugs thinking that having a good life just *is* having a sunnier disposition; another to think that having a sunnier disposition may be a necessary step toward living well. If you make the mistake of thinking about mood enhancement in the first way, you aren't likely to live well. You'll be like the heroin addict or the soma drinker, thinking that happiness is just feeling a certain way and foolishly adopting a totally passive view toward life.

If sales of SSRIs are any indication, the potential market for much more refined and effective mood enhancement drugs is enormous. So you can bet that we'll all be confronted, probably fairly soon, with the question of whether we ought to use them. It won't be the first time we'll be confronted with this kind of choice, of course. Long before there were SSRIs, there was alcohol, heroin, marijuana, cocaine, hashish, LSD, and hallucinogenic mushrooms. We already know that some people are vulnerable to misusing mood-enhancing drugs. But we also know that many people, in fact the majority, don't misuse them and that many don't use them at all.

Drug companies may eventually develop new mood enhancement drugs that are so effective that some people whom we don't now think of as having addictive personalities will misuse them. That's a possibility and we ought to be concerned about it. But once again we have to look at both sides of the ledger. Even if having a more positive temperament isn't living well, for many people it may make it more likely that they can live well. If many people would greatly benefit from mood enhancement drugs and wouldn't abuse them, would it be fair to ban them just because a minority of people will misuse them?

The answer to that question would depend on many factors. For one thing, on whether the misuse of the drug by the minority harmed other people. This certainly happens with the misuse of alcohol: Drunkenness is a major factor in car crashes, domestic violence, and work-related accidents, for example. Yet we still don't ban alcohol, partly because we respect the rights of those who don't abuse it and partly because we doubt that a ban would work and worry that it would have bad side effects (like organized crime during Prohibition).

It may turn out that science will provide a way of reducing the risk of mood enhancement drug abuse. Pharmacogenomics (PGx) is the science of understanding the connections between genes and reactions to drugs. With many drugs that are already on the market, there is a risk of adverse side effects, but not everybody is at risk, only a minority of users are. The problem is that until recently we haven't been able to know who will suffer adverse reactions until they occur. PGx can enable us to know in advance, if only those who have certain genes are liable to suffer the adverse side effect. The idea is to first do a genetic test before prescribing the drug. If the test shows that you are someone for whom the drug is dangerous (or merely ineffective), then you don't get the prescription.

This only works if there's a reliable gatekeeper: someone who will use the PGx information to make the decision whether you get the drug. Ordinarily, that's your doctor, but now it's possible to get PGx tests and other genetic tests without going through a doctor. You can order a test kit online. The test kit will arrive in the mail. It includes a questionnaire, a swab, and an envelope. You run the swab around the inside of your cheek and mail it along with the completed questionnaire back to the testing company and in a few days you get the results. Some of us will have enough self-control to get tested, either by our doctor or with a self-testing kit, before we take a mood enhancement drug, and to not take it if the test says that we are at risk for addiction or some adverse reaction.

Some won't. So we've still got a problem. As it turns out, a proposed solution is already on the table, but for the case of cocaine, not for new mood enhancement drugs. Here's the idea. Suppose it is possible to do a PGx test to determine who is at risk for cocaine addiction. Scientists already have developed a prototype cocaine vaccine. The vaccine is a drug that includes a big molecule that attaches itself to the cocaine molecule. This prevents the cocaine from passing the brain-blood barrier, which is a kind of filter that can prevent substances in the blood from getting into the brain. If the cocaine doesn't get to the brain, it doesn't produce the endorphins that contribute to addiction. Here's the catch: Some of the people, maybe many of them, who are at risk for addiction won't voluntarily get tested or take the vaccine. So there's a controversial public policy issue: Should testing be mandatory for everyone (or for everyone between, say, 12 and 60), and if you test positive, should vaccination be mandatory?

As more effective mood enhancement drugs become available we may have to face decisions like that. This much is certain: We need to start thinking hard, right now, about how to equip ourselves, as individuals and as a society, for coping with misuses of mood enhancement drugs. Good public policies probably won't be enough. We also need to think more clearly about some basic questions, including the question, what is happiness? Each of us also needs to ask ourselves whether we are likely to be able to use these drugs wisely. America already has a much more serious drug problem than most other developed countries. And it's overwhelmingly likely that America will be on the cutting edge when it comes to mood enhancement drugs. In the final chapter I'll explore some concrete ways to begin to prepare ourselves for the era of mood enhancement drugs and other biomedical enhancements.

I say prepare ourselves for it rather than avoid it, because I think that saying no to mood enhancement drugs is about as feasible as saying no to globalization. In both cases, we already have it and are almost certainly going to have more of it; the question is how to minimize the negatives and maximize the positives.

Moral Flabbiness

There's another character concern about enhancement drugs: the risk that their use will become a substitute for effort. Call this the Moral Flabbiness Problem. If you can take a pill to "achieve" some excellence, will it still be excellence? If we get in the habit of taking pharmaceutical shortcuts to our goals, won't our willpower atrophy?

Once again, this isn't a new problem. There's a drug called Alli that is marketed to overweight people. It makes the fat in what you eat congeal into globs that pass through your intestines and into the toilet. Because the fat goes right through you, you don't store it in your tissue. So, instead of needing to have enough willpower to avoid fatty foods, you only have to remember to take your Alli. Some people, including the members of Bush's Council, are very worried that biomedical enhancements will be shortcuts that lead to atrophy of our "moral powers." In fact, they are so worried that they think we should avoid enhancements—all of them, no matter how beneficial—altogether.

The worry about moral flabbiness is a serious issue, but we need to be careful about how we frame it. Sometimes shortcuts are perfectly fine. Consider your calculator or your GPS. It's probably true that people who rely exclusively on calculators are prone to the decay of their mathematical skills. Similarly, if GPS use becomes pervasive, there won't be as many people who have the traditional, low-tech skills I learned for my hiking merit badge. Once books became available, memory skills no doubt declined. The enhancement we call literacy no doubt contributed to the demise of epic oral poetry and the skills it required. That's no reason to abolish literacy.

It's true that if you "solve" a complex arithmetic problem using a calculator you don't accrue any credit for your mathematical ability. Similarly, you don't deserve praise for arriving successfully at a distant destination if you used your GPS. But it doesn't follow from that that you should throw away your calculator and your GPS. Life isn't a competition to see how much skill and effort you can exhibit for every task. Sometimes what matters is the result, not the process.

I wonder whether people who think the risk of moral flabbiness is so severe that we ought to avoid biomedical enhancements altogether are making a huge mistake: thinking that in a world of biomedical enhancements there is likely to be a *shortage* of opportunities for exerting willpower or effort. If that's what they're thinking, then they are overlooking an important fact, namely, that shortcuts typically lead to new opportunities for willpower and effort. Using your calculator or your GPS frees you to focus on doing things that are more important to you, and in most cases doing those more important things will involve exercise of the "moral powers" or other skills. A shortage of opportunities for exercising willpower and exerting effort is no more likely than the shortage of lack of control that Sandel worries about. The opportunity for exercising the moral powers isn't a fixed quantity that gets diminished every time you take a shortcut. Taking shortcuts typically opens up new opportunities.

This is especially obvious in the case of cognitive enhancements. If you get an enhancement of your cognitive powers, this doesn't mean that your ability to exert cognitive effort will atrophy. It means you're now able to undertake more complex, demanding cognitive tasks. The same is true for "performance-enhancing drugs." If you're one of the many musicians who take Adderall to steady your hands, I'll bet that you use this improvement to tackle more difficult pieces, not to make easy ones even easier. The enhancement serves as a higher platform from which you can exert efforts to attain new excellences.

I don't mean to underrate the risk of moral flabbiness. It will no doubt be a problem for some people. But the risk would have to be very pervasive to justify trying to avoid biomedical enhancements across the board. If the benefits of enhancements are great enough, the risk may be worth taking, especially if we can take reasonable steps to mitigate the risk.

Love Drugs

Some people who worry about the link between character and biomedical enhancement have another concern: They worry that the use of biomedical enhancements may result in inauthentic relationships. They're especially worried that in the future we may pop pills that will *seem* to enhance our relationships but will in fact result in different, inferior relationships.

Very recently, researchers have done some fascinating experiments that bear directly on this concern. They're experiments on voles, not humans, but their implications for us are mind-boggling. There are two species of voles that have radically different sexual behavior. One species is monogamous; the other is utterly undiscriminating in its choice of partners. Scientists have done an identity switch: They can turn the monogamous type into the promiscuous type and vice versa. They do this in either of two ways: by administering a drug (vasopressin for males, oxytocin for females) or by inserting genes from a member of one species into an embryo from a member of the other species. The same drugs are found naturally in humans, and humans also have similar genes. There's evidence that the chemicals in question play a role in human "pair-bonding."

We're not voles. It would be a mistake to assume that what can be done with them can be done with us. But these experiments and other research on the effects of chemicals on sexual behavior strongly suggest that at some point in the future we will be able to influence human sexual behavior by taking drugs designed for that purpose. Because sex (usually) plays a pretty central role in human pair-bonding, this means that it may become possible to enhance human pair-bonding by biochemical means.

Actually, we already do that, and have done it for thousands of years, using alcohol. Think of singles bars as low-tech pair-bonding facilities. In fact, there's now scientific evidence for what we've known all along: The more drinks you have, the lower your standards for attractiveness become. The experiment to test that hypothesis was simple: You show subjects photographs of members of the opposite sex, ask them to rate their attractiveness, and then see how the ratings are affected by increasing amounts of alcohol.

Remember the country music song lyric "I went home with a 10 at 2:00 and woke up with a 2 at 10:00"?

Humans have developed lots of other techniques for promoting pair-bonding by increasing sexual attractiveness: provocative clothing, walks on the beach at sunset, roses, and candlelit dinners. (The pair-bonding power of darkness should not be underestimated: Oscar Wilde once quipped, "Many a young man has made a proposal of marriage in lighting conditions under which he would not venture to purchase an inexpensive necktie." Or was it George Bernard Shaw?)

There are also a number of nonbiomedical techniques for *sustaining* the pair-bond: from vacations without the kids, to second honeymoons, to couples sex therapy. The state of Louisiana has a legal technique for sustaining pair-bonding. You can get married there in either of two ways: with a provision for no-fault divorce or with a fault-divorce option that imposes stiff financial costs on the one who is at fault. The second option is designed to provide a deterrent against infidelity.

Let's face it: Human pair-bonding is vulnerable to breakage. There are a number of temptations. Knowing that you'll lose your shirt if you yield to a temptation may make it considerably less seductive. Even with no-fault divorce, the fear of the economic loss that divorce brings may help some people stay together during rough patches; the Louisiana law simply ups the financial ante.

As our society changes, new threats to pair-bonding arise, but new techniques for combating them develop as well. Here's one example. Because the Internet makes it so easy to recontact old lovers, and because casual recontacts can sometimes lead to something more serious, some people simply follow a bright-line rule: no contacts with former lovers.

All of these nonbiomedical techniques for sustaining pair-bonding seem perfectly acceptable, from a moral point of view. In fact, using them seems morally admirable. It's a good thing to recognize your limitations and take reasonable steps to preserve what you value. Using them doesn't seem to indicate a character flaw; it only indicates that you admit that you aren't perfectly rational or a saint by nature. Maybe you'd be *more* virtuous if you didn't have to rely on them, but that doesn't mean it's bad to rely on them.

In a fascinating paper on "love drugs," Julian Savulescu and Anders Sandberg argue that there's nothing morally wrong about using drugs to enhance the normal human capacity for pair-bonding. I agree. Yet in spite of my effort to convince you that enhanced pair-bonding isn't new, you may have reservations. In particular, you may worry whether a relationship that was sustained by chemical means was *authentic*.

The first thing to notice is that this way of framing the issue is misleading. Savulescu and Sanderg aren't proposing that drugs alone would ensure the survival of the relationship. That's too biologically deterministic. Their idea is that we may get to a point where carefully designed drugs can make it *more likely* that a couple will stay together. In other words, it's not a question of a pair-bonding pill anymore than of a music appreciation pill in Sanjay's case. The biomedical enhancement in both cases isn't a substitute for effort; it merely increases the odds that your effort will pay off. Still, you may be worried that the use of the drug makes the relationship inauthentic, even if the drug alone isn't sustaining it. Would it still be love?

That's a badly framed question, for two reasons. First, the term "love" is notoriously slippery. Different cultures have different conceptions of love, and even within the same culture there can be different conceptions of love. Even within our society we disagree about what real love is. Once we specify what we mean by love, we need to ask another question: Is love even relevant in all cases in which the issue of enhanced pair-bonding would arise? If by love you mean romantic love, then many people around the world who value stable marriages or long-term relationships may be quite unconcerned about whether chemical enhancements are compatible with love. For them, romantic love isn't necessary for a good relationship. Second, Savulescu and Sandberg aren't claiming that taking a drug like vasopressin or oxytocin can by itself *create* a long-term relationship, much less a long-term relationship that is loving. The idea, rather, is that if you have a loving relationship, you may be able to increase its chances of survival by taking the drug (assuming that you are doing lots of other things to try to preserve it).

In trying to figure out whether the drug is a threat to the authenticity of the relationship, it's important to avoid a big mistake: thinking that by taking the drug we are *introducing* chemicals into the pair-bonding situation. Chemicals—the same chemicals—are already there and, according to evolutionary psychologists, are already playing a role in pair-bonding. So the choice isn't between chemically enhanced pair-bonding and "natural" pair-bonding. The choice isn't drugs versus no drugs. It's the *deliberate* use of drugs versus taking your chances with whatever levels of them you happen to have as a result of your individual body chemistry.

Deliberately taking the same chemicals that already play a role in human pair-bonding would rob the relationship of authenticity if they *compelled* you and your mate to stay together. At least with some understandings of love, compulsion of *that sort* is incompatible with love. But notice, if the worry is that compulsion would undermine authenticity, we've slipped from the realm of scientifically based speculation to macabre fantasy—the world of the *Valley of the Dolls* or, more grimly, of serial killer Jeffrey Dahmer, who injected battery acid into the skulls of his victims in a rather unscientific attempt to make them his love slaves. Let's not go there; we're supposed to be talking about pair-bonding enhancement drugs, not love zombie fantasies.

In spite of everything I've said so far, I imagine that some people will still say that the *natural* biochemical contribution to pair-bonding is just fine, but the deliberate use of the same chemicals is inauthentic or in some other way wrong. Authentic relationships, they might say, are based on our given biological nature. Taking enhancement drugs interferes with that nature.

This line of thinking is hopelessly enmeshed in the old, pre-Darwinian view of nature. Remember, from chapter 1, what John Stuart Mill said about nature? Nature either means the whole natural world, that is, everything that's not supernatural, including us and whatever we do, including biomedical enhancement; or it means what would happen if we didn't take any action. Given the way evolution works, there's good reason to think that nature in the first sense doesn't always get it right and that therefore it's often appropriate for us to "interfere" with nature in the second sense—that is, to take action so that we get outcomes that wouldn't occur if we didn't act. That's why diabetics take insulin, why we evacuate areas where tsunamis are headed, etc.

As it turns out, there's reason to believe that so far as human pair-bonding goes, things are often not optimal if we refrain from taking serious measures to sustain the bond. Many evolutionary biologists believe that human males are especially prone to sexual infidelity, as a result of their evolved characteristics. The idea is that males have evolved to have a strong tendency to spread their genes around. If that's true, then evolution has created an obstacle to achieving what we value: a stable relationship. If what we value is a stable relationship and if male infidelity is an obstacle to that, then perhaps we ought to "interfere" with nature and do something to try to counteract this unfortunate tendency.

Some psychologists are suspicious of gene-focused explanations of the fact that on average males are more prone to infidelity than females. They think that the difference may be that males, who are generally more physically powerful and who also tend to have more social power, are more likely to be unfaithful because they can more often get away with it. Regardless of whether the explanation of male infidelity is biological or cultural, or some combination of the two, if you're a male who values a stable relationship and who believes (quite reasonably) that infidelity is a risk to stability, you ought to think of ways to counteract the risk. There's no reason to take pair-bonding enhancement drugs off the table. If they are available and safe, they deserve serious consideration.

Any strategy for sustaining a relationship, whether it involves the deliberate administration of drugs or not, may carry risks. For example, if you opt for a fault-divorce marriage contract with severe economic penalties for the one at fault, you might end up stuck in a very bad situation. Suppose that the person you married degenerates into someone you would never think of marrying (or turns out to have been bad from the first but was very good at disguising this fact). Now you're in a fix: You can't free yourself of him without incurring economic disaster. In the case of the deliberate use of pair-bonding enhancement drugs, there could also be the risk of bad physical side effects, as there is with virtually all drugs.

There might also be the risk, for some people, of overreliance—that's the moral flabbiness problem we encountered earlier. Some people might put too much stock in the enhancement drug and not devote enough effort to other things that are essential for sustaining a relationship. This risk isn't unique to enhancements. It comes with medicines—drugs to prevent or treat diseases—as well. The weight-reduction drug Alli is one example; here are two more. If you go to a dialysis clinic, you may actually see people who are currently undergoing dialysis eating foods that are strictly forbidden for people with bad kidneys—salty potato chips, for example. If you ask them why they're doing that, they may say, "Oh, it won't hurt anything; I might have to go to dialysis a little more often, but it's worth it." Similarly, some people who take Lipitor to keep their cholesterol down eat more fatty foods than they would if they couldn't rely on the medicine. Does that mean we should ban dialysis and Lipitor?

Do We Need to Enhance Our Character?

Physician-bioethicist Thomas Douglas is just completing a fascinating dissertation on moral enhancement. His work is directly relevant to the concern that the availability of biomedical enhancements may be corrupting—that it may either lead to a worsening of our character or at least give greater scope for us exhibiting character flaws we already have. People who think that the character risk of enhancement is so great that we should avoid enhancement altogether have a pretty pessimistic view of our character. They think we aren't strong enough to resist the temptations that enhancements will bring. If that's true, then perhaps we should think more about how we could improve our character. Douglas considers a number of possibilities for moral enhancement drugs. His discussion is sophisticated and somewhat technical. I won't try to replicate or even summarize it here. Instead, I'll draw on it and supplement it with some thoughts of my own, in order to show that the idea of moral enhancement makes sense.

From an evolutionary standpoint, it would be surprising if we were able to cope with the new challenges that biomedical enhancements present, without enhancing ourselves. Our distinctively human biology was shaped largely during the Pleistocene, 100,000 or 150,000 years ago, by an environment that was radically different from the world you and I live in. We've already developed some ways of enhancing our moral performance: You can view religion and ethics that way. We've also developed institutions, like the law, that can help us behave better. Perhaps we need further moral enhancements and perhaps some of them will be biomedical.

How would that work? There are two main possibilities. Both are highly speculative. I think they're much less speculative, however, than the prediction that the risk that enhancement poses to our character is so overwhelming that we should try to abstain from all enhancements!

One the one hand, some *cognitive* enhancements might help us be more virtuous. Sometimes, how well we behave depends on what we know. Virtues, remember, are complex dispositions and include the ability to make sound judgments about what's right and wrong. In some cases, making sound judgments requires mastery of fairly complex facts and the ability to reason, to draw valid conclusions from premises. We already know that children and early adolescents aren't very good at making some decisions because they aren't very good at thinking about the future consequences of their acts. Adults might also be capable of improvement in this regard.

Memory-improving drugs might also contribute to our being better morally. Most of us think that truthfulness is a virtue. But given how fallible human memory is, it's a very hard virtue to have. To the extent that we value truth—and want to try to avoid the vice of self-deception—we ought to be concerned about the fallibility of our memories. In other words, if you care about truth, you ought to care about having a better memory. Biomedical enhancements of memory could be not only useful, but also morally obligatory.

There's yet another way that cognitive enhancements might have good moral effects. Psychologists have shown that human beings are prone to certain cognitive errors, mistakes in reasoning. Some of these mistakes can contribute to patterns of behavior that are traditionally called vices. Here's one example: We tend to be too quick to attribute other people's behavior to their personalities, not taking seriously enough the influence of environmental factors. This cognitive bias can lead to unfair judgments about others and self-serving attitudes about ourselves. If we developed safe biomedical means for helping to combat this kind of error, it would be a good thing.

So far, we've considered how cognitive enhancements could make us better morally. Enhancing our moral emotions might also make us morally better. Sympathy and empathy are moral emotions. Virtuous people are sympathetic and empathetic. If we come to understand the biochemical and neurological bases of the moral emotions, we may be able to enhance them. We might be able to improve our capacity for moral imagination—for vividly entertaining possibilities other than the status quo, or for fully appreciating the impact of our actions on others.

We already use nonbiomedical techniques to try to improve moral imagination. For example, when I teach a course on human rights, I have students watch a documentary that personalizes the Holocaust by including interviews with survivors who describe what happened to them and their families. The documentary also makes the horrors more vivid by showing graphic film footage of what Allied soldiers found when they liberated the death camps in the spring of 1945. Perhaps moral imagination can be improved through education. Perhaps education isn't enough and needs a biomedical boost. Again, it's not a matter of biomedical intervention substituting for doing the hard work of cultivating moral sentiments; the question is whether there is a supporting role for biomedical interventions.

These possibilities for moral improvement through biomedical means don't assume biological determinism. The idea isn't that we'll be able to pop moral virtue pills or have an empathy tissue implant in our brains. It's a more modest idea: that to the extent that moral virtues have a biological substrate, we may be able to improve them by modifying the biology.

If you think that's far-fetched, consider what I call *moral glucose loading*. Psychologists have documented the phenomenon of moral decision-making fatigue. If you have to make a series of moral decisions in a fairly short time, your decision-making capacity deteriorates. They've also shown that the deterioration can be counteracted to some extent, by increasing the levels of glucose in your brain. Glucose is something that our brains already have. Why would it make any moral difference if instead of glucose we used some new substance, produced by drug research, to have the same effect?

I mentioned earlier that our ability to be morally good may be limited by our evolved nature. Some evolutionary biologists think that we have an evolved tendency toward xenophobia—fear of strangers—and outright hostility toward them. Having this psychological tendency might have been a good thing for survival when we lived in small hunter-gatherer bands and there was no law and order. It may be very bad for us now. I don't see how we can rule out the possibility that we may eventually learn how to diminish this nasty tendency through the use of biomedical technologies. I'm not suggesting that biomedical interventions alone would do the trick. The idea, rather, is that a biomedical intervention might be one aspect of a multifaceted effort to extend concern and respect to all human beings, not just those who are like us.

The more general point is this: If you think we should avoid enhancements because you think our present character is so flawed that we are bound to misuse them, you're assuming that our character is fixed. It may not be.

I began this chapter with an attempt to cut through the over-heated rhetoric of Michael Sandel's assault on enhancement. What's distinctive about Sandel's approach is his focus on character. I've tried to show that there are a number of different worries about the relationship between enhancement and character. It's much more complex than his categories of the drive for mastery and openness to the unbidden suggest. I've also tried to show that none of these character concerns amounts to an "argument against enhancement," if that means a compelling reason for trying to refrain from enhancements altogether. Character concerns aren't "arguments against enhancement," but they are something we have to take very seriously. Contrary to what Sandel says, there's no problem with enhancement *as such*—enhancement per se doesn't "represent" anything problematic. What particular enhancements "represent" will depend on the particular circumstances. But there are lots of ways you can go wrong in pursuing enhancements and some of them have to do with character.

7 | THE ENHANCEMENT ENTERPRISE

We've gone a considerable distance since we encountered Michelle's and Carlos's knee-jerk reactions to enhancement in chapter 1. We've seen that matters are more complicated than they thought. It's worth the effort to try to summarize the main conclusions of our investigation, even if doing so will inevitably involve oversimplification.

- Biomedical enhancements are already here and more are on the way, whether we like it or not. Research to cure and prevent disease will inevitably open up new possibilities for being better than well, for increasing human capacities by biomedical means. So 'just saying no' isn't an option.
- The age of biomedical enhancements will bring new challenges, but it's a mistake to think that the ethical problems are novel. This isn't surprising given that enhancement is a very old human activity—indeed a distinctively human activity, something that helps define us. The risks include lack of appreciation for what we have, "hyperparenting," unwittingly making things worse in an attempt to improve them, and worsening existing injustices. But none of these are new problems. They arise whenever human beings attempt to improve their condition or that of their children.

- What matters most is how we prepare ourselves for meeting the challenges that biomedical enhancements will bring. The first step is to rid ourselves of false framing assumptions and faulty metaphors that can bias our decisions about enhancement.

- Nature or evolution is not like a master engineer. The natural—the biological status quo—is rarely optimal, and sometimes it's not even acceptable. To make a rational evaluation of the possibilities of biomedical enhancement, we have to rid ourselves of pre-Darwinian, romanticized, rosy assumptions about nature and our own biology. Human nature is a mixed bag, with plenty of room for improvement.

- It's a mistake to assume that the various elements of human nature are so densely interconnected that any attempt to improve it will be disastrous. The more we learn about how we are put together, the better equipped we'll be for selectively and safely intervening to make improvements. Sweeping generalizations about seamless webs are unhelpful. We need more fine-grained knowledge of causal connections. We need cautionary rules of thumb solidly grounded in knowledge of causal connections. As our knowledge increases, interventions that would now be foolish will become reasonable. Any sane approach to the risks of biomedical enhancement must be knowledge-sensitive, and this means it must both reflect and encourage the growth of knowledge.

- Attempts to draw bright lines that exclude biomedical enhancements across the board fail. It makes no sense to draw a bright line between enhancement and the cure or prevention of disease. Sometimes, there are good reasons to go beyond therapy, to try to be better than well. Our concepts of health and disease are tied to what we think is natural for us, but what is natural for us is merely a reflection of where we happen to be now, as a result of our evolutionary development. Evolution doesn't create products that are biologically optimal, much less optimal from the standpoint of what we rightly value. Even if it's true that the aim of medicine is health, that doesn't show that it's wrong to use biotechnologies to make us better than well. A "well" elderly person, for example, has stiff, painful joints, reduced libido, compromised mental functioning, and poor physical stamina. If we can safely use biotechnologies to reduce some of the afflictions of old age, we should do so, and, morally speaking, it doesn't matter whether this counts as treatment or enhancement.

- Reflections on human nature can't tell us whether any particular biomedical enhancement is advisable or inadvisable, right or wrong. At most, human nature serves as a constraint on what can be good or right for us; it shapes the general character of morality and flourishing for us. Even that may change, however, because what have been constraints up until now may be relaxed by biomedical interventions.

- In the enhancement debate, as elsewhere, appeals to human nature and the natural are risky. The best minds have often made serious mistakes about what's part of human nature and what isn't. Even worse, talk about human nature and the natural is often stealth moral imperialism: passing off highly subjective moral views as if they were statements of fact. In addition, talk about human nature and the natural is often used to stigmatize, demean, and marginalize certain people. In the ethics of enhancement, as in ethics generally, everything of value that can be framed in the language of human nature and the natural can be said just as well without using those terms, and with less risk of confusion and abuse.

- Enhancement isn't the pursuit of perfection or total mastery. In some cases people may pursue enhancements out of an unseemly desire for mastery or because they fail to properly appreciate what they have. But it's simply false to say that enhancement "represents" the desire for mastery or the pursuit of perfection. People can and do have different motives, and mixed motives, for enhancement. In this respect, biomedical enhancements are no different from the traditional enhancements, like education and science. To take biomedical enhancements off the table on the basis of a wild prediction that they will inevitably involve mass delusions of total control is not only hysterical; it's ethically irresponsible.

- The risks to character that biomedical enhancements pose are not new risks: They arise for every human endeavor at improvement. If history is any indication, we can be reasonably confident of two points about this risk. First, in some cases, it will be worth running, because the benefits will be great enough. Second, the risk will not be equally distributed; some people will abuse biomedical enhancements and some won't, just as some people now abuse prescription drugs or alcohol or cosmetic surgery and most don't. In the case of biomedical enhancements that will bring great benefits to many people and that will not be abused by most, we should be very cautious about banning them simply because some people will abuse them.

- Biomedical enhancement raises serious issues of justice, but none of them are new issues. They arise for all previous enhancements—from agriculture to literacy, numeracy, computers, and the development of institutions—in brief, for all valuable innovations. Instead of indulging in biomedical enhancement exceptionalism, we need to think about the more general problem of justice in the diffusion of valuable innovations. Drawing on information about the conditions under which valuable innovations diffuse rapidly, we need to ensure that valuable biomedical enhancements quickly become available to all who want them.

To do this will require institutional innovation, including, perhaps, modifications of intellectual property rights.

- The proper focus is not equality in the distribution of biomedical enhancements. Here, as elsewhere, equality is not of much, if any value in itself. What matters is: (1) avoiding inequalities that result in domination, exploitation, and exclusion, and (2) harnessing biomedical enhancements and other valuable innovations to reduce deprivation. The view that nobody should have an enhancement unless everybody can have it is just as absurd and morally repugnant as the view that nobody should be literate or have indoor plumbing or enough to eat unless everybody does.

- Much of the current debate about justice issues has been distorted by false framing assumptions about what sort of goods enhancements will be: that they will be expensive, zero-sum, personal goods, provided exclusively through the market. These assumptions overlook the fact that some of the most valuable biomedical enhancements will bring social benefits, and not just to those who possess them; that they will enable new forms of highly productive and rewarding cooperation; that governments may regard them as valuable enough to encourage or subsidize; and that their costs are likely to decrease over time, as with computers, cell phones, and prescription drugs when they go off patent.

- It is a serious mistake to think that the benefits of biomedical enhancements are limited to their direct benefits to those who have them. Some biomedical enhancements, including improvements in cognition and moral enhancements, will be of broad social benefit. This is true, in particular, of enhancements that are characterized by network effects and those that increase productivity. Overlooking the fact that enhancements can bring great social benefits stacks the deck against enhancements, pushing us toward an overly conservative or negative attitude toward them.

- Once we appreciate that some biomedical enhancements will bring broad social benefits, including increased productivity, we must abandon the comforting assumption that the risk of state-driven eugenics is a thing of the past. Government subsidization of biomedical enhancement may ease some of the problems of distributive justice, but it also raises the specter of mandatory enhancements.

The Enhancement Enterprise: Front Door Versus Back Door Enhancement

We've already crossed the threshold of the age of biomedical enhancement. This is hardly surprising, given the sort of creatures we are. Human beings are niche-constructors par excellence: We repeatedly alter our environment to suit our needs and preferences. In doing this we inevitably alter ourselves as well. The new environments we create alter our social practices, our cultures, our biology, and even our identity. In other words, given that the environment we shape in turn shapes us, our niche-construction inevitably involves self-reconstruction. The only difference now is that for the first time we can *deliberately*, and in a *scientifically informed way*, change our selves.

As I argued in chapter 2, because of problems that result from our altering our environment, we may have to undertake biomedical interventions—for example, to cope with emerging pandemics or the effects of toxins in the environment or global warming. We may also have to undertake biomedical interventions to cope with some of the flaws in our biological design—for example, to correct for natural selection's insensitivity to problems that arise as we age.

Finally, we may want to use biotechnologies to enhance certain capacities simply because doing so will improve our lives. Once we discard the fiction that the way we are now is permanent and optimal, we ought to take the possibilities of enhancement seriously.

I haven't tried to make a blanket "Case for Enhancement." Frankly, that would be stupid. Some enhancements—for some people, in some circumstances, if undertaken for certain reasons—will be a good idea, and some will be bad. We have to resist the urge for sweeping generalizations, for the false comfort of blanket endorsement or rejection. I do think I've succeeded in showing that efforts to make a "Case Against Enhancement" fail. There's no good reason to try to refrain from biomedical enhancements altogether.

The fact that we shouldn't reject biomedical enhancement across the board doesn't mean that anything goes. We've got to learn to think in a more nuanced way that recognizes all the complexities. But we also have to make a choice, and we must make it very soon. We have to decide whether we're going to continue to let enhancements slip in the back door, willy-nilly, or whether we are going to embark on what I call the enhancement enterprise.

Embarking on the enhancement enterprise means allowing considerable freedom to private individuals and organizations to develop and choose to use enhancement technologies, including biomedical enhancement technologies. It also means devoting significant public resources to research that can be expected to result in enhancement technologies *and* to create a vigorous and informed public debate about the benefits and risks of such technologies. Just as important, it means developing effective and morally sensitive policies and institutions for coping with the challenges of enhancement.

A society that engages in the enhancement enterprise recognizes the *legitimacy* of biomedical enhancement, as one mode of enhancement among others, both as a personal aim that individuals may permissibly pursue and as a permissible kind of policy goal that must compete for public resources with other permissible policy goals. In its public policy, such a society rejects the view that biomedical enhancement per se is illegitimate, either because it is *enhancement*, rather than the treatment or prevention of disease, or because it uses *biomedical* technology or involves biological changes. By recognizing enhancement, including biomedical enhancement, as a legitimate aim, it implicitly rejects the ill-founded, sweeping generalization that the pursuit of enhancement betrays morally unacceptable motivations or bad character.

When a society undertakes the enhancement enterprise it thereby rejects the anti-enhancement position, the view that biomedical enhancements are to be avoided altogether. More positively, it commits itself to developing the moral and institutional resources needed to pursue enhancements responsibly.

Recognizing enhancement as a legitimate aim for individuals and for social policy makes a great deal of difference. It changes the way deliberations about biomedical enhancements are framed. One of the most important framing shifts is that now biomedical enhancement must compete fairly and openly with other social goals in the process of allocating resources. In contrast, in a society in which biomedical enhancement comes in through the back door, piggybacking on the treatment and prevention of disease, ever-greater amounts of social resources may flow to it but without any opportunity for democratic, scientifically informed decisions about how valuable it is compared with other goals. Acknowledging the legitimacy of biomedical enhancements takes the "no enhancements" alternative off the table, so far as social policy is concerned. But in doing so it *increases* our ability to say no to particular biomedical enhancements, either by prohibiting their use or by refusing to support their development with public funding.

A final point about the notion of legitimacy is worth making. Regarding biomedical enhancement as a legitimate social aim doesn't imply that all individuals are expected to agree that it *is* an appropriate aim for social policy, much less that all must regard it as something they ought to undertake for themselves or their children. In any pluralistic society, there will be some legitimate social policy aims that are rejected by some citizens. Engaging in the enhancement enterprise means giving individuals considerable freedom *not* to pursue enhancements.

At some point, however, the implementation of a social policy aimed at achieving widespread use of a particular biomedical enhancement may come into conflict with some individuals' values. This is nothing new, of course. For example, educational policies and policies regarding medical care and compulsory vaccination for children sometimes conflict with parental preferences and values.

In my judgment, it will probably be quite a long time before we have biomedical enhancements that are both powerful enough and safe enough for it to make sense to develop social policies to try to ensure their large-scale use. For the foreseeable future, pursuing the enhancement enterprise will largely consist of trying to make good decisions on four issues. (1) How many resources ought to be devoted to research on various types of enhancements? (2) How can such research be conducted safely and ethically? (3) How can we effectively monitor the effects of enhancements that are being used, either as spin-offs from treatment and prevention of disease or explicitly as enhancements? (4) How can we reliably identify which enhancements are safe and effective, and make them more accessible to those who want them and could benefit from them?

One aim of this book has been to try to determine whether the most serious worries about biomedical enhancement—even if they are insufficient to rule out enhancement across the board—give us good reason to refrain from embarking on the enhancement enterprise. My answer is: No, not at present anyway. But I also hope I've made a strong case for a more positive claim: There are powerful reasons in favor of a society like ours embarking on the enhancement enterprise, and there are no objections to enhancement that are sufficient to outweigh them, at least at the present time.

There are several reasons in favor of the enhancement enterprise. First, once we get beyond the dubious assumptions that enhancements will be predominantly zero-sum competitive goods or expressions of bad character, it becomes clear that the potential social benefits of pursuing the enhancement enterprise are great. Second, the risks of living in a society in which enhancements continue to come in through the back door, as new applications of treatment technologies, or through research conducted in countries with inadequate controls on human experimentation, are unacceptably high, given the alternative of pursuing the enhancement enterprise. A third advantage of pursuing the enhancement enterprise is that doing so would facilitate institutional efforts to control enhancements in the name of justice, such as proposals for modifying intellectual property rights like the one I sketched in chapter 6. Fourth, recognizing the legitimacy of enhancement avoids inappropriate medicalization: Once we recognize the legitimacy of enhancement as a familiar and admirable human activity, there's no need to pretend that biomedical interventions that are really aimed at enhancement are treatments of diseases. That reduces the unfortunate tendency to multiply maladies without good reason.

At present, to get legal access to cognitive enhancement drugs, you have to convince physicians (and perhaps yourself as well) that you have a disease—attention deficit disorder, narcolepsy, Alzheimer's dementia, or some other cognitive disorder. There's a lot to be said for being in a society where efforts to improve our capacities don't require us to view every gap between the way we are now and the way we desire to be as evidence of disease.

Consider the case of therapeutic drugs now being used for cognitive enhancement in people who are cognitively normal. Where enhancement is not recognized as legitimate, those with the money to pay black market prices or the social connections and education to persuade physicians to prescribe Ritalin or other drugs "off label" will have access; others will not. Ironically, prohibiting enhancements out of fear that they will only be available to the rich exacerbates problems of distributive injustice. In a society that recognizes the legitimacy of enhancement, new regulatory institutions can be developed to facilitate the wider and more rapid diffusion of highly beneficial and safe enhancements, in part by eliminating overmedicalization.

Those who worry about unintended bad medical or social consequences of enhancement should endorse the enhancement enterprise. We're much more likely to make reasonable judgments about the risks of various enhancements if we can subject them to regulatory scrutiny and political debate. Consider the case of Michelle's use of cognitive enhancement drugs. Like a growing number of other students, Michelle is engaging in an uncontrolled, unmonitored experiment. Stanford bioethicist Henry Greely and his colleagues have argued persuasively that the use of such drugs for enhancement should be studied in large-scale, long-term, clinical trials. This is not likely to occur in any systematic way, so long as enhancement is viewed as illegitimate. The hardest work in the ethics of enhancement can begin once we've reached a consensus that biomedical enhancement can be a legitimate and even noble kind of activity.

REFERENCES

Agar, Nicholas. (2004). *Liberal Eugenics: In Defence of Human Enhancement.* (Malden, MA: Wiley-Blackwell).

Amundson, R. (1994). "Two Concepts of Constraint: Adaptationism and the Challenge from Developmental Biology." *Philosophy of Science* 61: 556–78.

Amundson, R., and G. Lauder. (1994). "Function Without Purpose: The Uses of Causal Role Function in Evolutionary Biology." *Biology and Philosophy* 9: 443–69.

Anderson, Elizabeth. (1999). "What Is the Point of Equality?" *Ethics* 109: 287–337.

Annas, George. (1998). "Why We Should Ban Human Cloning." *New England Journal of Medicine* 339: 122–25.

Annas, George. (2002). "Cell Division." *Boston Globe.* April 21, E1–2.

Annas, George. (2005). *American Bioethics: Crossing Human Rights and Health Law Boundaries.* (Oxford: Oxford University Press).

Atkins, D. C., D. H. Baucom, and N. S. Jacobson. (2001). "Understanding Infidelity: Correlates in a National Random Sample." *Journal of Family Psychology* 15(4): 735–49.

Babcock, Linda et al. (1995). "Biased Judgments of Fairness in Bargaining." *American Economic Review* 85(5): 1337–43.

Baillie, Harold W., and Timothy K. Casey, eds. (2004). *Is Human Nature Obsolete? Genetics, Bioengineering, and the Future of the Human Condition.* (Cambridge, MA: MIT Press).

Bales, K. L., W. A. Mason, C. Catana, et al. (2007). "Neural Correlates of Pair-Bonding in a Monogamous Primate." *Brain Research* 1184: 245–53.

Beatty, J. (1984). "Pluralism and Panselectionism." *Philosophy of Science Association.* P. D. Asquith and P. Kitcher, eds. (East Lansing, MI: The University of Chicago Press on behalf of the Philosophy of Science Association).

Beitz, Charles R. (2009). *The Idea of Human Rights*. (Oxford: Oxford University Press).

Bloom, D. E., D. Canning, and J. Sevilla. (2004). "The Effect of Health on Economic Growth: A Production Function Approach." *World Development* 32(1): 1–13.

Bloom, D. E., D. Canning, and M. Weston. (2005). "The Value of Vaccination." *World Economics* 6: 15–39.

Bostrom, N. (2004). "The Future of Human Evolution." *Death and Anti-Death: Two Hundred Years After Kant, Fifty Years After Turing*. Charles Tandy, ed. (Palo Alto, CA: Ria University Press), pp. 339–71.

Bostrom, N. (2008). "Smart Policy: Cognitive Enhancement in the Public Interest." *Reshaping the Human Condition: Exploring Human Enhancement*. Leo Zonneveld, Huub Dijstelblowem, and Danielle Ringoir, eds. (The Hague, Netherlands and London: Rathenau Institute, British Embassy Science & Innovation Network, and Parliamentary Office of Science and Technology), pp. 29–36.

Bostrom, N., and Rebecca Roache. (2009). "Smart Policy: Cognitive Enhancement and the Public Interest." *Enhancing Human Capacities*. J. Savulescu, R. T. Meulen and G. Kahane, eds. (Oxford: Wiley Blackwell).

Bostrom, N., and A. Sandberg. (2009). "The Wisdom of Nature: An Evolutionary Heuristic for Human Enhancement." *Human Enhancement*. Julian Savulescu and Nick Bostrom, eds. (Oxford: Oxford University Press).

Boyd, Robert, and Joan Silk. (2006). *How Humans Evolved*. (New York: W. W. Norton and Co.).

Brand, R. J., C. M. Markey, A. Mills, and S. D. Hodges. (2007). "Sex Differences in Self-Reported Infidelity and Its Correlates." *Sex Roles* 57: 101–9.

Brandon, R. N. (2006). "The Principle of Drift: Biology's First Law." *Journal of Philosophy* CIII(7): 319–35.

Brandon, R. N., and M. D. Rausher. (1996). "Testing Adaptationism: A Comment on Orzack and Sober." *The American Naturalist* 148(1): 189–201.

Brennan, Geoffrey, and Alan Hamlin. (2004). "Analytic Conservatism." *British Journal of Political Science* 34: 675–92.

Brennan, Geoffrey, and Philip Pettit. (2004). *The Economy of Esteem*. (New York: Cambridge University Press).

Brighouse, Harry, and Adam Swift. (2006). "Equality, Priority, and Positional Goods." *Ethics* 116: 471–97.

Brock, Dan. (1995). "The Non-Identity Problem and Genetic Harms—The Case of Wrongful Handicaps." *Bioethics* 9(3): 269–75.

Brock, Dan. (2003). "Ethical Issues in the Use of Cost-Effectiveness Analysis for the Prioritization of Health Care Resources." *Making Choices in Health: WHO Guide to Cost-Effectiveness Analysis.* T. Edejer et al., eds. (Geneva: World Health Organization), pp. 289–312.

Buchanan, Allen. (1984). "The Right to a Decent Minimum of Health Care." *Philosophy & Public Affairs* 13(1): 55–78.

Buchanan, Allen. (1996). "Is There a Medical Profession in the House?" *Conflicts of Interest in Clinical Practice and Research*. David Schimm et al., eds. (Oxford: Oxford University Press), pp. 105–36.

Buchanan, Allen. (1996). "Toward a Theory of the Ethics of Bureaucratic Organizations." *Business Ethics Quarterly* 6: 419–40.

Buchanan, Allen. (2004). *Justice, Legitimacy, and Self-Determination: Moral Foundations for International Law*. (Oxford: Oxford University Press).

Buchanan, Allen. (2008). "Enhancement and the Ethics of Development." *Kennedy Institute Journal of Ethics* 18: 1–34.

Buchanan, Allen. (2009). "Human Nature and Enhancement." *Bioethics* 23(3): 141–50.

Buchanan, Allen. (2009). "Philosophy and Public Policy: A Role for Social Moral Epistemology." *Journal of Applied Philosophy* 26(3): 276–90.

Buchanan, Allen. "Moral Status and Enhancement." unpublished paper.

Buchanan, Allen, Dan W. Brock, Norman Daniels, and Daniel Wikler. (2001). *From Chance to Choice: Genetics and Justice*. (New York: Cambridge University Press).

Buchanan, Allen, Tony Cole, and Robert O. Keohane. (forthcoming). "Justice in the Diffusion of Innovation." *Journal of Political Philosophy*.

Bull, Hedley. (1977). *The Anarchical Society*. (New York: Columbia University Press).

Buss, Leo. (1987). *The Evolution of Individuality.* (Princeton, NJ: Princeton University Press).

Christiano, Thomas. (2008). *The Constitution of Equality: Democratic Authority and Its Limits.* (Oxford: Oxford University Press).

Ciliberti, S., O. Martin, and A. Wagner (2007). "Innovation and Robustness in Complex Regulatory Gene Networks." *PNAS* 104(34): 13591–96.

Cohen, G. A. "Rescuing the Truth in Conservatism." unpublished paper.

Daniels, Norman. (2001). "Justice, Health, and Healthcare." *The American Journal of Bioethics* 1(2): 2–16.

Daniels, Norman. (2009). "Can Anyone Really Be Talking About Modifying Human Nature?" *Human Enhancement.* Julian Savulescu and Nick Bostrom, eds. (Oxford: Oxford University Press), pp. 25–42.

Darwall, Stephen. (2006). *The Second-Person Standpoint: Morality, Respect, and Accountability* (Cambridge, MA: Harvard University Press).

Dawkins, Richard. (1976). *The Selfish Gene.* (Oxford: Oxford University Press).

Dawkins, Richard. (1999). *The Extended Phenotype: The Long Reach of the Gene* (Oxford: Oxford University Press).

Dawkins, Richard. (2003). *A Devil's Chaplain: Reflections on Hope, Lies, Science, and Love.* (New York: Houghton Mifflin Harcourt).

DeCamp, Matthew. (2007). "Global Health: A Normative Analysis of Intellectual Property Rights and Global Distributive Justice." PhD Dissertation. Duke University.

DeGrazia, David. (2000). "Prozac, Enhancement and Self-Creation." *Hastings Center Report* 30(2): 34–40.

De Waal, Franz. (2006). *Primates and Philosophers: How Morality Evolved.* S. Macedo and J. Ober, eds. (Princeton, NJ: Princeton University Press).

Diamond, Jared. (1997). *Guns, Germs and Steel: The Fates of Human Societies.* (New York: W.W. Norton and Co.).

Douglas, Thomas. (2008). "Moral Enhancement." *Journal of Applied Philosophy* 25(3): 228–45.

Douglas, Thomas, and Katrien Devolder. "Wide Procreative Beneficence: Beyond Individualism in Reproductive Selection." unpublished manuscript.

Elliot, Carl. (1998). "The Tyranny of Happiness." *Enhancing Human Traits: Ethical and Social Implications.* Erik Parens, ed. (Washington, DC: Georgetown University Press), pp. 177–88.

Ereshefsky, Marc. (2007). "Where the Wild Things Are: Environmental Preservation and Human Nature." *Biology and Philosophy* 22: 57–72.

Erler, Alexandre. (2012). "Authenticity and the Ethics of Self-Change." PhD Dissertation. University of Oxford.

Faust, Halley. (2008). "Should We Select for Genetic Moral Enhancement? A Thought Experiment Using the MoralKinder (MK+)." *Theoretical Medicine and Bioethics* 29(6): 397–416.

Fay, J. C., G. J. Wyckoff, and C. I. Wu. (2001). "Positive and Negative Selection on the Human Genome." *Genetics* 158: 1227–34.

Fenton, Elizabeth, and John D. Arras. (2010). "Bioethics and Human Rights: Curb Your Enthusiasm." *Cambridge Quarterly of Health Care Ethics* 19: 127–33.

Fogel, Robert W. (2004). *The Escape from Hunger and Premature Death, 1700– 2100: Europe, America, and the Third World.* (New York: Cambridge University Press).

Frank, Robert. (2001). *Luxury Fever*, new ed. (Princeton, NJ: Princeton University Press).

Frankel, Mark S. (2003). "Inheritable Genetic Modification and a Brave New World." *Hastings Center Report* 33(2): 31–36.

Friedman, Benjamin M. (2005). *The Moral Consequences of Economic Growth.* (New York: Alfred A. Knopf).

Fukuyama, Francis. (2003). *Our Posthuman Future: Consequences of the Biotechnology Revolution.* (London: Profile Books).

Galvani, A. P., and M. Slatkin. (2003). "Evaluating Plague and Smallpox as Historical Selective Pressures for the CCR5-Delta 32 HIV Resistance Allele." *Proc. Natl. Acad. Sci. USA* 100: 15276–79.

Gardiner, S. M. (2006). "A Core Precautionary Principle." *Journal of Political Philosophy* 14(1): 33–60.

Gibson, G., and G. Wagner. (2000). "Canalization in Evolutionary Genetics: A Stabilizing Theory?" *Bioessays* 22(4): 372–80.

Giles, Jr., Egbert Leigh. (1971). *Adaptation and Diversity: Natural History and the Mathematics of Evolution*. (San Francisco: Freeman, Cooper & Company).

Glover, Jonathan. (2003). *Choosing Children: Genes, Design, and Disability*. (Oxford: Oxford University Press).

Goldin, C., and C. Rouse. (2000). "Orchestrating Impartiality: The Impact of 'Blind' Auditions on Female Musicians." *American Economic Review* 90(4): 715–41.

Grant, Ruth, and Robert O. Keohane. (2005). "Accountability and Abuses of Power in World Politics." *American Political Science Review* 99(1): 29–43.

Greeley, Henry, Barbara Sahakian, John Harris, Ronald C. Kessler, Michael Gazzaniga, Philip Campbell, and Martha J. Farah. (2008). "Towards Responsible Use of Cognitive-Enhancing Drugs by the Healthy." *Nature* 456: 702–5.

Ha, Michael N., Frank L. Graham, Chantalle K. D'Souza, William J. Muller, Suleiman A. Igdoura, and Herb E. Schellhorn. (2004). "Functional Rescue of Vitamin C Synthesis Deficiency in Human Cells Using Adenoviral-Based Expression of Murine L-Gulono-Γ-Lactone Oxidasestar." 83(3): *Genomics* 482–92.

Habermas, Jurgen. (2003). *The Future of Human Nature*. (Cambridge: Polity).

Haller, J., E. Mikics, J. Halasz, and M. Toth. (2005). "Mechanisms Differentiating Normal from Abnormal Aggression: Glucocoricoids and Serotonin." *European Journal of Pharmacology* 526(1–3): 89–100.

Harris, John. (2007). *Enhancing Evolution* (Princeton, NJ: Princeton University Press).

Heidegger, Martin. (1993). "The Question Concerning Technology." *Basic Writings*. D. F. Krell, ed. (New York: HarperCollins).

Hirschman, Albert O. (1991). *The Rhetoric of Reaction: Perversity, Futility, Jeopardy*. (Cambridge, MA: The Belknap Press).

Hull, David. (1986). "On Human Nature." *Philosophy of Science Association. 2(A)*. A. Fine and P. Machamer, eds. (East Lansing, MI: Philosophy of Science Association), pp. 3–13.

Hume, David. (1983). *An Enquiry Concerning the Principles of Morals*. 1777 ed. J. B. Schneewind, ed. (Indianapolis, IN.: Hackett Pub. Co.).

Insel, T. R., and R. D. Fernal. (2004). "How the Brain Processes Social Information: Searching for the Social Brain." *Annual Review of Neuroscience* 27: 697–722.

Jones, G. (2008). "Are Smarter Groups More Cooperative? Evidence from Prisoner's Dilemma Experiments, 1959–2003." *Journal of Economic Behavior and Organization* 68(3–4): 489–97.

Kass, Leon. (1997). "The Wisdom of Repugnance." *New Republic* 216(22): 17–26.

Kass, Leon. (2003). "Ageless Bodies, Happy Souls." *The New Atlantis* 1: 9–28.

Kass, Leon. (2004). "L'Chaim and Its Limits: Why Not Immortality?" *The Fountain of Youth: Cultural, Scientific, and Ethical Perspectives on a Biomedical Goal*. Stephen Post and Robert Benstock, eds. (New York: Oxford University Press).

Keohane, Robert O. (1989). *International Institutions and State Power* (Boulder, CO: Westview).

Kingsbury, Benedict, Nico Krisch, and Richard Stewart. (2005). "The Emergence of Global Administrative Law." *Law and Contemporary Problems* 68(3–4): 15–62.

Kirk, Russell. (2001). *The Conservative Mind: From Burke to Eliot*. 7th ed., revised. (Washington, DC: Regnery Publishing).

Klingenberg, C. P. (2008). "Morphological Integration and Development of Modularity." *Annual Review of Ecological Evolutionary Systems* 39: 115–32.

Krasner, Stephen D., ed. (1983). *International Regimes*. (Cambridge, MA: MIT Press).

Landes, David S. (2003). *The Unbound Prometheus: Technological Change and Industrial Development in Western Europe from 1750 to the Present*. (New York: Cambridge University Press).

Lehrman, D. (1953). "A Critique of Konrad Lorenz's Theory of Instinctive Behavior." *The Quarterly Review of Biology* 28: 337–63.

Lewontin, R. C. (1982). "Organism & Environment." *Learning, Development, Culture*. Henry Plotkin, ed. (New York: Wiley), pp. 151–70.

Lim, Miranda et al. (2004). "Enhanced Partner Preference in a Promiscuous Species by Manipulating the Expression of a Single Gene." *Nature* 429(6993): 754–57.

Machery, E. (2008). "A Plea for Human Nature." *Philosophical Psychology* 21: 321–30.

McCabe, Sean Esteban, John R. Knight, Christian J. Teter, and Henry Wechsler. (2005). "Non-Medical Use of Prescription Stimulants Among US College Students: Prevalence and Correlates from a National Survey." *Addiction* 99: 96–106.

McMahan, Jeff. (2004). *The Ethics of Killing: Problems at the Margins of Life.* (Oxford: Oxford University Press).

McMahan, Jeff. (2009). "Cognitive Disability and Cognitive Enhancement." *Metaphilosophy* 40(3–4): 582–605.

McNeil, J. (2001). *Something New Under the Sun: An Environmental History of the Twentieth-Century World.* (New York: W. W. Norton & Co.).

Mill, John Stuart. (1904). "On Nature." *Nature, The Utility of Religion and Theism.* (London: Watts & Co.).

Murray, Thomas. (2007). "Enhancement." *Oxford Handbook of Bioethics.* B. Steinbock, ed. (New York: Oxford University Press), pp. 491–515.

Neander, K. (1991). "Functions as Selected Effects: The Conceptual Analyst's Defense." *Philosophy of Science* 58: 168–84.

Nijhout, H. F. (2003). "The Control of Growth." *Development* 130(24): 5863–67.

Odling-Smee, J. J., K. N. Laland, and M. W. Feldman. (2003). *Niche Construction: The Neglected Process in Evolution.* (Princeton, NJ: Princeton University Press).

O'Keane, V., E. Moloney, H. O'Neill, A. O'Connor, C. Smith, and T Dinan. (1992). "Blunted Prolactin Responses to D-fenfluramine in Sociopathy. Evidence for Subsensitivity of Central Serotonergic Function." *The British Journal of Psychiatry* 160(5): 643–46.

Orzack, S. H., and E. Sober. (1994). "How (Not) to Test an Optimality Model." *Trends in Ecology and Evolution* 9: 265–67.

Parens, Erik. (1995). "The Goodness of Fragility: On the Prospect of Genetic Technologies Aimed at the Enhancement of Human Capacities." *Kennedy Institute of Ethics Journal* 5(2): 141–53.

Parens, Erik, ed. (1998). *Enhancing Human Traits: Ethical and Social Implications.* (Washington, DC: Georgetown University Press).

Parfit, Derek. (1986). *Reasons and Persons.* (New York: Oxford University Press).

Paul, Diane. (2005). "Genetic Engineering and Eugenics: The Uses of History." *Is Human Nature Obsolete?* Harold W. Baillie and Timothy K. Casey, eds. (Cambridge, MA: MIT Press), pp. 123–52.

Persson, Ingmar, and Julian Savulescu. (2008). "The Perils of Cognitive Enhancement and the Urgent Imperative to Enhance the Moral Character of Humanity." *Journal of Applied Philosophy* 25(3): 162–77.

Pinker, Steven. (2003). *The Blank Slate: The Modern Denial of Human Nature.* (New York: Penguin).

Pontius, Anneliese A. (1982). "Face Representation Linked with Literacy Level in Colonial American Tombstone Engravings and Third World Preliterates' Drawings. Toward a Cultural-Evolutionary Neurology." *Cellular and Molecular Sciences* 38: 577–81.

Powell, R. (2010). "The Evolutionary Biological Implications of Human Genetic Engineering." *Journal of Medicine and Philosophy.* doi: 10.1093/jmp/jhq004.

Powell, R., and Allen Buchanan. (2011). "Breaking Evolution's Chains: The Promise of Enhancement by Design." *Enhancing Human Capacities.* Julian Savulescu, ed. (Oxford University Press). doi: 10.1093/jmp/jhq057.

President's Council on Bioethics. (2002). *Beyond Therapy.* (Washington, DC: National Bioethics Advisory Commission).

President's Council on Bioethics. (2003). *Human Cloning and Human Dignity: An Ethical Inquiry.* (Washington, DC: National Bioethics Advisory Commission).

Richerson, Peter, and Robert Boyd. (2005). *Not by Genes Alone: How Culture Transformed Human Evolution.* (Chicago, IL: University of Chicago Press).

Ridley, Matt. (2003). *Nature via Nurture: Genes, Experience, and What Makes Us Human*. (New York: Harper Collins).

Rio Declaration on Environment and Development. UN Doc. A/CONF. 151/26 (vol. I); 31 ILM 874 (1992).

Ruse, M. (2003). *Darwin and Design: Does Evolution Have a Purpose?* (Cambridge, MA: Cambridge University Press).

Sandberg, Anders. (forthcoming). "The Economics of Cognitive Development." *Enhancing Human Capacities*. Julian Savulescu et al., eds. (Oxford: Wiley-Blackwell Publishers).

Sandberg, Anders, and Nick Bostrom. (2006). "Converging Cognitive Enhancements." *Ann. N.Y. Acad. Sci.* 1093: 201–27.

Sandel, Michael. (2004). "The Case Against Perfection: What's Wrong with Designer Children, Bionic Athletes, and Genetic Engineering?" *The Atlantic Monthly* 292(3): 51–62.

Sandel, Michael. (2007). *The Case Against Perfection: Ethics in the Age of Genetic Engineering*. (Cambridge, MA: Harvard University Press).

Sansom, Roger. (2003). "Constraining the Adaptationism Debate." *Biology and Philosophy* 18: 493–512.

Savulescu, Julian. (2006). "Justice, Fairness, and Enhancement." *Annals of the New York Academy of Sciences* 1093(1): 321–38.

Savulescu, Julian, and Anders Sandberg. (2008). "Neuroenhancement of Love and Marriage: The Chemicals Between Us." *Neuroethics* 1(1): 33–44.

Scanlon, T. M. (1998). *What We Owe to Each Other*. (Cambridge, MA: The Belknap Press).

Schroeder, E. Todd et al. (2007). "Hormonal Regulators of Muscle and Metabolism in Aging (Horma): Design and Conduct of a Complex, Double Masked Multicenter Trial." *Clinical Trials* 4(5): 560–71.

Scruton, Roger. (2001). *The Meaning of Conservatism*. 3rd ed. (South Bend, IN: St. Augustine's Press).

Sober, Elliott. (1984). *The Nature of Selection: Evolutionary Theory in Philosophical Focus*. (Cambridge, MA: MIT Press).

Sreenivasan, Gopal. (2002). "International Justice and Health: A Proposal." *Ethics and International Affairs* 16: 81–90.

Steinbock, Bonnie. (2008). "Designer Babies: Choosing Our Children's Genes." *Lancet* 372(9646): 1294–95.

Tishkoff, S. A., F. A. Reed, A. Ranciaro, et al. (2007). "Convergent Adaptation of Human Lactase Persistence in Africans and Europeans." *Nature Genetics* 39(1): 31–40.

Tversky, A., and D. Kahneman. (1981). "Framing Decisions and the Psychology of Choice." *Science* 211(4481): 453–58.

Waldron, Jeremy. (2002). *God, Locke, and Equality: Christian Foundations in Locke's Political Thought.* (Cambridge: Cambridge University Press).

Walker, Mark. "Genetic Virtue." unpublished manuscript.

Walzer, Michael. (1983). *Spheres of Justice: A Defense of Pluralism and Equality.* (New York: Basic Books).

Weinstein, I. B. (2002). "Addiction to Oncogenes—the Achilles Heal of Cancer." *Science* 297: 63–64.

Wells, Spencer. (2002). *The Journey of Man: A Genetic Odyssey.* (Princeton, NJ: Princeton University Press).

Wikler, Daniel I. (1979). "Paternalism and the Mildly Retarded." *Philosophy & Public Affairs* 9: 377–92.

Wikler, Daniel I. (2009). "Paternalism in the Age of Cognitive Enhancement: Do Civil Liberties Presuppose Roughly Equal Mental Ability?" *Human Enhancement.* Julian Savulescu and Nick Bostrom, eds. (Oxford: Oxford University Press), pp. 341–55.

Wingspread Statement on the Precautionary Principle. (1998). http://www.gdrc.org/u-gov/precaution-3.html.

INDEX